BEAUTY PRIME

Celebrating the Visionaries of Beauty

beautyprime.co.uk
ISSUE: 4 - 2024
GLOBAL EDITION

CONFIDENCE IS THE FOUNDATION OF TRUE BEAUTY

The Power Of Fashion And Makeup In Building Self-Confidence

PASCALE ROTHMAN
Redefines health with integrity, transparency, and innovation

MELINDA NICCI
Empowers Women Through Wellness

KRISTIAN EDWARDS
Empowers Wellness

Editor's Picks

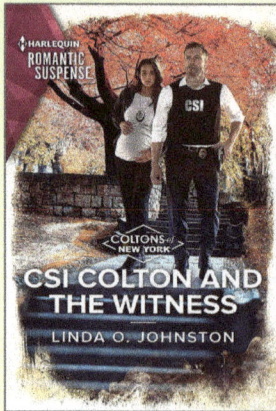

CSI Colton and the Witness

LINDA O. JOHNSTON

"Linda O. Johnston masterfully blends romance and suspense, creating a thrilling narrative that keeps readers on the edge of their seats."

Paperback: £6.95

https://amzn.to/4hQlWtz

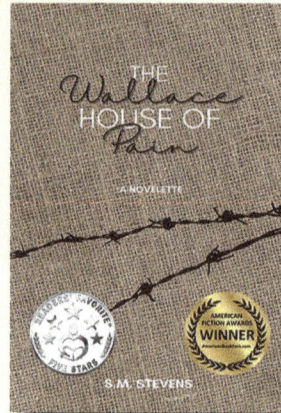

The Wallace House of Pain

S.M. STEVENS

"A compelling exploration of family dynamics and social justice, delivering a powerful message of acceptance and self-discovery."

Kindle: £2.39

https://amzn.to/4ezKDaL

Merely Mortal

MICHELLE M. PILLOW

A thrilling urban fantasy romance, "Merely Mortal" captivates with its supernatural intrigue, dynamic characters, and unexpected twists. Must-read!

Paperback: £15.46

https://amzn.to/40Otkzt

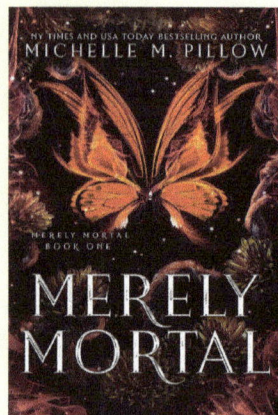

Change of Heart

CRISTINA LEPORT

"Change of Heart" is a riveting medical thriller, expertly blending suspense, crime, and medical intrigue. A must-read page-turner!"

– Margaret Earing,

Hardcover £21.99

https://amzn.to/3SjkhSb

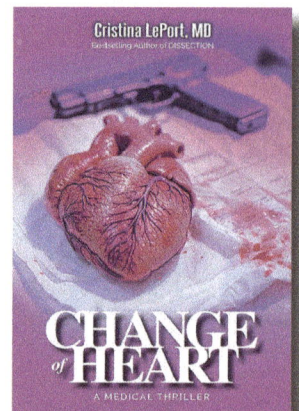

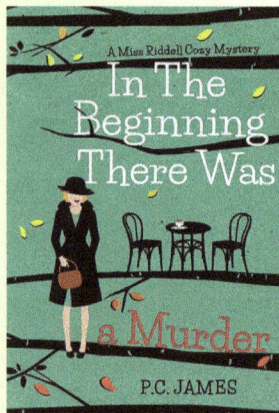

In The Beginning, There Was a Murder

P.C. JAMES

"In The Beginning, There Was a Murder" is a gripping cozy mystery with twists, smart heroine, and 1950s intrigue. Must-read!

Papperback: £9.99

https://amzn.to/3OgDaTr

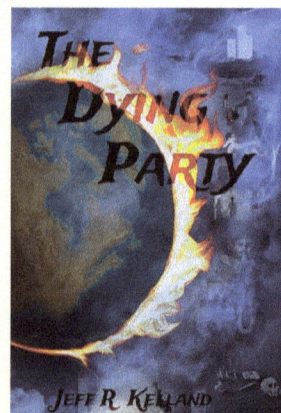

The Dying Party

JEFF KELLAND

"The Dying Party explores a future where climate change is unstoppable, following both the poor and elite's survival struggles."

Kindle: £2.14

https://amzn.to/3CuFmE9

Words Whispered in Water

SANDY ROSENTHAL

"Words Whispered in Water" reveals Sandy Rosenthal's battle to uncover the truth behind Hurricane Katrina's levee failures, challenging powerful entities."

Paperback: £10.50

https://amzn.to/4fwsJqT

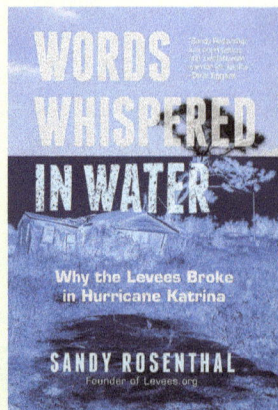

Midnight Marriage

LUCINDA BRANT

"Midnight Marriage" follows Julian's secret quest to win Deb's heart, set in the lavish Georgian aristocracy.

paperback: £9.99

https://amzn.to/3UUkbl6

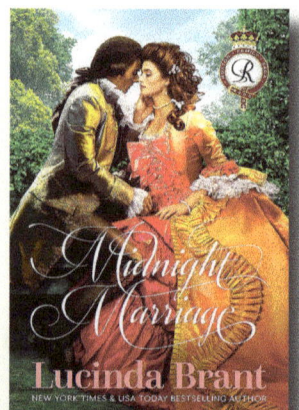

Your Gateway to Endless Stories

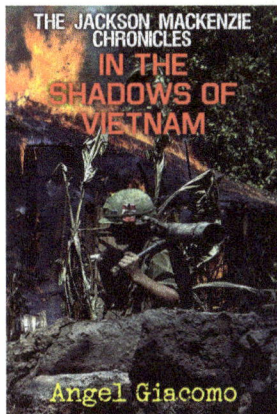

The Jackson MacKenzie Chronicles
ANGEL GIACOMO
"A gripping tale of courage and resilience", "In the Shadows of Vietnam" masterfully captures the Vietnam War's intense challenges.

– Steven Setil

Kindle: £2.95

https://amzn.to/40UZnxN

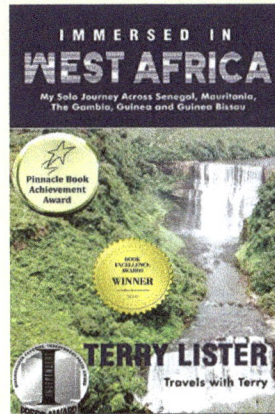

Immersed in West Africa
TERRY LISTER
"Immersed in West Africa" by Lister is a captivating exploration of diverse cultures, offering profound insights and inspiring connections through its vivid storytelling and adventurous spirit.

Paperback: £7.49

https://amzn.to/4hPOjbp

Fairy Tale Science
SARAH ALBEE
"*Fairy Tale Science* by Sarah Albee brilliantly blends fantasy and facts, making science enchanting and accessible for curious young minds."

Hardcover: £14.99

https://amzn.to/3Od7nTf

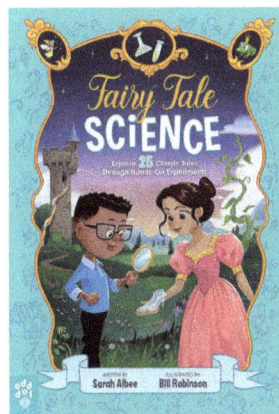

The Darkest Passages
LEN HANDELAND
"The Darkest Passages" captivates with its intense blend of passion, revenge, and supernatural intrigue, delivering a thrilling vampire saga.

Hardcove: £14.54

https://amzn.to/3UVUErW

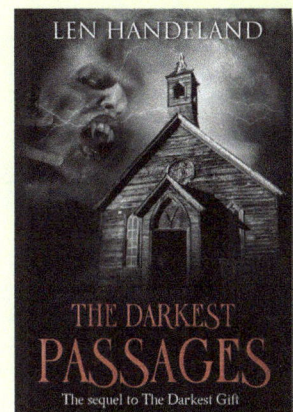

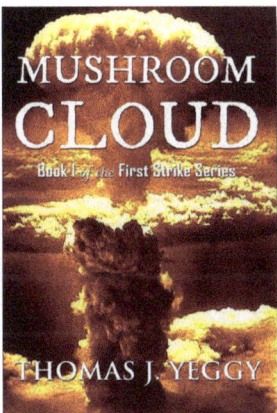

Mushroom Cloud
THOMAS J. YEGGY
"Mushroom Cloud" masterfully blends historical fact with gripping fiction, offering a compelling narrative on nuclear disarmament's critical importance.
Paperback: £7.99

https://amzn.to/3YUALCJ

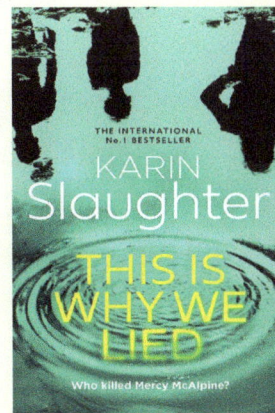

The Midnight Man
JULIE ANDERSON
"The Midnight Man" captivates with its atmospheric post-war London setting and clever mystery, featuring determined female sleuths.

Paperback: £10.99

https://amzn.to/3zTe4pF

Defiance Passage
TERRY OVERTON
"Defiance Passage" follows brave teens in a dystopian world, seeking freedom and knowledge while evading oppressive forces. Adventure awaits!

Paperback: £10.24

https://amzn.to/3ZazCrV

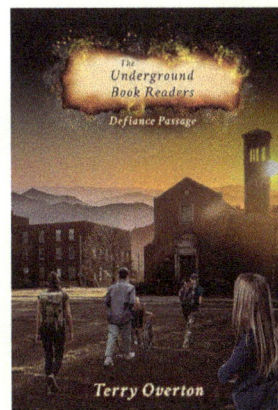

You Will Never Be Me
JESSE SUTANTO
"As an influencer's life unravels, jealousy and revenge take center stage in this suspenseful tale filled with unexpected twists and dark humor.
Paperback: £9.73

https://amzn.to/3O9UtFI

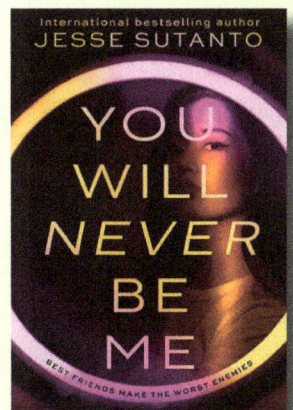

SPRING TREES, 24 X 30 by Janet H. Dilenschneider

A vibrant celebration of renewal, this painting captures the essence of spring with its lively colors and dynamic composition, inviting viewers to experience the rejuvenating energy of nature's awakening.

What's INSIDE

Issue 4 -2024

PUBLISHER: Beauty Prime, A Subsidiary of NewYox Media Group. 200 Suite 134-146 Curtain Road, EC2A 3AR London, United Kingdom t: +44 79 3847 8420 editor@beautyprime.co.uk II http://beautyprime.co.uk

EDİTORIAL: Ben O'Leory, Editor-in-Chief, Heater Turner, Managing Editor, C. Rochelle, Art Editor, Lyra Green, Content Editor, Reporters: Jack Wilson, Jenny Taylor , J. Evans, Amy Browm, Ben F. Oncu CONTRIBUTOS: Claudine D. Reyes, Adrian T.

We assume no responsibility for unsolicited manuscripts or art materials provided from our contributors.

From the Editor's Desk

Welcome to the fourth issue of *Beauty Prime* magazine! As we step into a new year, we are thrilled to bring you another edition filled with inspiration, creativity, and thought-provoking stories. At *Beauty Prime*, we believe that beauty is not just about appearances—it's about confidence, resilience, and the power of self-expression.

In this issue, we explore the artistry of aesthetics, the transformative power of storytelling, and the intersection of culture and innovation. From Sarah Barker's insights into the artistry of beauty to Pascale Rothman's redefinition of health with integrity, our contributors continue to inspire and challenge conventional norms.

Our *Editor's Picks* section highlights a diverse range of books that promise to captivate and engage readers. Whether it's the suspenseful twists of Linda O. Johnston's *CSI Colton and the Witness*, the gripping historical fiction of Thomas J. Yeggy's *Mushroom Cloud*, or the empowering journey through West Africa with Terry Lister, there's something for everyone to discover.

We also delve into the world of art and culture, featuring the works of Sofia Ruiz, David Osbaldeston, and Jungmin Lee, who explore memory, emotion, and beauty in their unique ways. In literature, we celebrate the creative brilliance of authors like Sherry Argov, Marlene Bell, and Cheryl Burman, who continue to redefine storytelling and inspire readers worldwide.

At *Beauty Prime*, we are committed to showcasing voices that empower, uplift, and challenge us to see the world through new perspectives. This issue is a testament to the incredible talent and passion of our contributors, editors, and readers.

As always, we welcome your feedback and ideas. Your support and engagement fuel our mission to celebrate beauty in all its forms. Thank you for being a part of our journey.

Here's to a year of confidence, creativity, and endless possibilities!

Warm regards,

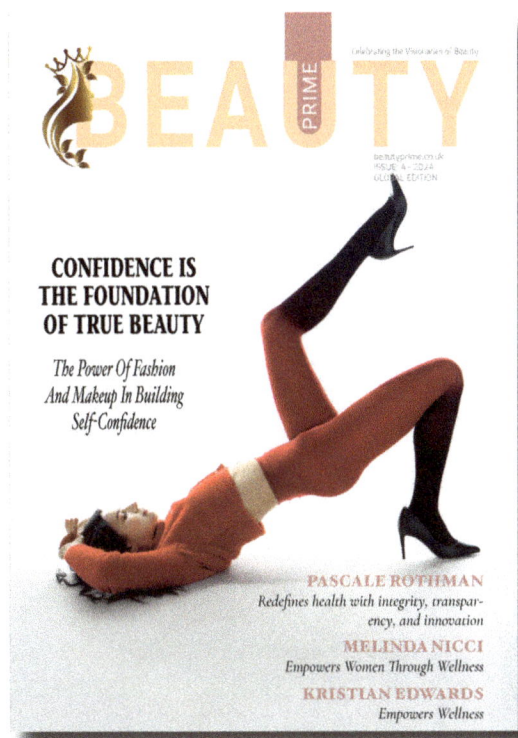

CONFIDENCE IS THE FOUNDATION OF TRUE BEAUTY

The Power Of Fashion And Makeup In Building Self-Confidence

PASCALE ROTHMAN
Redefines health with integrity, transparency, and innovation

MELINDA NICCI
Empowers Women Through Wellness

KRISTIAN EDWARDS
Empowers Wellness

"A Soft Spot" by Sofia Ruíz, 2024. This captivating oil and acrylic piece on canvas (76.2 x 101.6 cm) invites viewers to explore the delicate interplay of color and emotion.

Yana Barabash discusses her artistic journey, the influence of the Isle of Wight, her creative process, and her approach to life coaching, emphasizing the importance of finding joy in the present.

SOFIA RUIZ

Exploring the Boundaries of Creativity and Self-Discovery

as told to Jenny Taylor

Sofia Ruiz stands as a beacon of artistic innovation and cultural exploration, her work resonating deeply with audiences around the globe. Born in San José, Costa Rica, Sofia embarked on her artistic journey at the tender age of 16, driven by a profound sense of isolation and a longing for connection. Her early experiences, marked by personal challenges, have profoundly shaped her creative vision, infusing her art with themes of psychoanalysis, duality, and memory. With a degree in Painting and Printmaking from the School of Fine Arts in Costa Rica and a Master's in Education, Sofia has not only honed her craft but also enriched her understanding of art as a medium for communication and healing. Her impressive portfolio includes over 35 exhibitions worldwide and participation in international residencies from the USA to South Korea, each experience adding a unique layer to her artistic narrative. Sofia's work is a visual diary that explores identity and the influence of family, offering viewers a chance to reflect on their own emotional landscapes. Her accolades, including several national and international art awards, underscore her impact and dedication to her craft.

In this exclusive interview for Mosaic Digest Magazine, Sofia Ruiz opens up about her artistic journey, the interplay between painting and printmaking in her work, and the cultural influences that have shaped her thematic focus. She

A Soft Spot Oil and Acrylic on canvas
76,2 x 101,6 cm 2024

The Aloof Artist_Oil on canvas
61 x 61 cm_2024

LadyBird_oil on canvas
61 x 61 cm_

shares insights into the significant moments of her career, the role of education in her artistic practice, and the universal messages she hopes to convey through her art. Join us as we delve into the mind

> Sofia Ruiz masterfully blends emotion and technique, creating art that resonates universally and inspires introspection across cultural boundaries.

of this extraordinary artist, whose work continues to inspire and connect people across diverse cultural contexts.

Your journey as an artist began at the age of 16 in San José, Costa Rica. What initially drew you to the world of art, and how did those early experiences shape your style and creative vision?

I started drawing at five because my father gave me small notebooks and a pen to keep me occupied while we waited to see my mother. She suffered from temporary amnesia for a few years, and I think that, along with the lack of photographs from my childhood, influenced me significantly. During that time, I felt disconnected from my family; my mother didn't recognize me, and my father was often working. Those feelings of isolation and longing for

connection became integral to my artistic drive.

At 16, I began looking for art through tattoo magazines and tried to copy designs, and I realized that drawing came naturally to me. As I grew, art helped me find the sense of belonging I was missing. These experiences sparked my interest in psychoanalysis, duality, and memory, which later shaped my creative vision. My work has become a visual diary exploring my identity and how family influences who we are. It's also a healing process that continues to evolve.

In 2007, you majored in Painting and Printmaking from the School of Fine Arts in Costa Rica. How do these mediums complement each other in your work, and what influences your choice between them for different projects?

Printmaking offers many techniques and materials to explore. I appreciate the complexity of processes like etching, which involve trial and error. Painting, on the other hand, allows for spontaneity and immediate expression. Working in both mediums has taught me to balance exploration with the freedom that painting offers.

When I want to layer ideas carefully, I choose printmaking. But when I want to express something raw and intuitive, I turn to painting. These two mediums complement each other, allowing me to maintain

a dynamic creative process between structure and freedom.

You have participated in international residencies from the USA to South Korea. How have these experiences in different cultures influenced your artistic process and thematic focus?

Each residency has broadened my understanding of how art operates in different cultural contexts. Some exposed me to new ways of blending technology with traditional printmaking, encouraging experimentation. Engaging with artists from diverse backgrounds has been particularly enriching because you can see how our cultures influence how we view things through a different lens.

As an award-winning artist with over 35 exhibitions globally, what do you consider the most significant moments in your career so far, and how have they impacted your approach to art?

A meaningful moment was my first solo exhibition, where I felt both excited and exposed.

Every opportunity to show my work feels significant, whether in a small gallery or a museum. In Costa Rica, opportunities can feel limited, so seeing my work appreciated abroad has been incredibly rewarding.

Winning the Best Overseas Artist Prize at the Women in Art Prize in London was another important moment. These experiences have helped build my confidence to con-

tinue creating, even in challenging times.

In addition to your artistic practice, you hold a Master's in Education. How has your background in education influenced the way you engage with your work, and do you see a connection between teaching and creating?

Teaching has helped me simplify complex ideas, which influences my art. Both art and teaching involve breaking down intricate concepts like identity into relatable expressions, facilitating a deeper connection with the viewer. Both teaching and creating are ways of understanding and sharing ideas, helping me express them in a clearer, more accessible way.

What message or emotion do you hope viewers take away from your work, especially considering the diverse cultural contexts you engage with in your exhibitions around the world?

I hope viewers feel a sense of introspection when they engage with my work. I often explore themes of fragmentation, identity, and memory, and I want people to leave with a deeper understanding of their emotional layers. The ultimate message is that our experiences, though complex and fragmented, leave traces that connect us all. I explore the duality of identity: how we define ourselves versus how others perceive us. This theme resonates universally, regardless of cultural context.

> " A Bold Statement Of
> Confidence And Style:
> Beauty Prime
> Magazine's Cover
> Reflects Empowerment
> Through Fashion And
> Self-Expression.

CONFIDENCE IS THE FOUNDATION OF TRUE BEAUTY

The Power Of Fashion And Makeup In Building Self-Confidence

By Lyra Green

This article explores how beauty transcends physical appearance, focusing on confidence, self-expression, and individuality through fashion, makeup, and personal style, empowering individuals to embrace their uniqueness and redefine beauty standards.

In a world where beauty is often equated with physical appearance, it's easy to forget that true beauty transcends the surface. It's not just about flawless skin, perfect hair, or the latest fashion trends. True beauty is deeply intertwined with confidence and self-expression—the ability to embrace who you are and project that authenticity to the world. When we shift our focus from external validation to internal empowerment, we unlock a version of beauty that is not only timeless but also transformative.

THE CONNECTION BETWEEN BEAUTY AND CONFIDENCE

Confidence is the foundation of beauty. It's the invisible force that makes someone stand out in a crowd, regardless of their physical attributes. When you feel confident, it radiates through your posture, your smile, and the way you carry yourself. This inner glow is far more captivating than any makeup product or designer outfit.

But where does this confidence come from?

For many, it's rooted in self-acceptance and the freedom to express themselves authentically. Beauty, in this sense, becomes a tool for self-expression rather than a standard to conform to. It's about celebrating your individuality and using fashion, makeup, and personal style as mediums to tell your unique story.

FASHION AS A FORM OF EMPOWERMENT

Fashion is one of the most powerful ways to express confidence. The clothes we wear are more than just fabric; they are statements of who we are and how we want to be perceived. A bold leather jacket, a tailored suit, or a flowing dress can all convey different aspects of our personality. The key is to choose pieces that make you feel good about yourself.

For example, someone might feel empowered in a pair of thigh-high boots and a sleek bodysuit, as seen in the *Be-

Continued *on page 20*

"Confidence Is the foundation of beauty."

auty Prime* magazine cover. These choices exude boldness and self-assurance, sending a message that the wearer is unapologetically themselves. On the other hand, someone else might find confidence in a minimalist outfit that emphasizes simplicity and elegance. The beauty of fashion lies in its versatility—it allows everyone to find their own voice.

MAKEUP AS A TOOL FOR SELF-EXPRESSION

Makeup is another powerful tool for building confidence. It's not about hiding imperfections or meeting societal standards; it's about enhancing your natural features and expressing your mood or creativity. A swipe of red lipstick can make you feel bold and fearless, while a soft, dewy look can evoke a sense of calm and grace.

The act of applying makeup can also be a form of self-care. Taking the time to focus on yourself, even for a few minutes, can be incredibly grounding. It's a ritual that allows you to connect with your inner self and prepare to face the world with confidence. Whether you prefer a full glam look or a bare-faced glow, the choice is yours—and that's where the power lies.

PERSONAL STYLE: THE ULTIMATE CONFIDENCE BOOSTER

Personal style is the intersection of fashion, beauty, and individuality. It's about curating a look that feels authentic to you, rather than trying to fit into a mold. When you embrace your personal style, you're telling the world, "This is who I am, and I'm proud of it."

Developing a personal style takes time and experimentation. It's a journey of self-discovery that involves trying new things, making mistakes, and learning what works for you. Along the way, you'll find that the more you align your outward appearance with your inner self, the more confident you'll feel.

BREAKING FREE FROM BEAUTY STANDARDS

One of the biggest obstacles to confidence is the pressure to conform to unrealistic beauty standards. These standards, perpetuated by media and advertising, often make people feel like they're not good enough. But the truth is, beauty is not one-size-fits-all. It's diverse, dynamic, and deeply personal.

By rejecting these standards and embracing your unique features, you can redefine what beauty means to you. This shift in perspective is incredibly liberating. It allows you to focus on what makes you feel beautiful, rather than what others expect of you.

THE ROLE OF SELF-ACCEPTANCE

At the heart of beauty and confidence is self-acceptance. This means acknowledging your flaws and imperfections, not as shortcomings, but as part of what makes you human. It's about being kind to yourself and recognizing that you are enough, just as you are.

Self-acceptance doesn't happen overnight. It's a process that requires patience and practice. But once you start to see yourself through a lens of compassion rather than criticism, you'll find that confidence comes naturally. And with confidence, your beauty will shine brighter than ever.

BEAUTY AS A JOURNEY, NOT A DESTINATION

Ultimately, beauty and confidence are not destinations to be reached but journeys to be embraced. They evolve as you grow and change, reflecting the different stages of your life. What makes you feel beautiful today might not be the same as what made you feel beautiful a year ago—and that's okay. The important thing is to stay true to yourself and continue exploring what makes you feel confident and empowered.

In conclusion, beauty is so much more than skin deep. It's about confidence, self-expression, and the courage to be yourself. Whether through fashion, makeup, or personal style, you have the power to define your own beauty and share it with the world. So go ahead—embrace your uniqueness, celebrate your individuality, and let your confidence shine. After all, there's nothing more beautiful than being unapologetically you.

Unveiling the Artistry of Aesthetics with
SARAH BARKER

Discover Sarah Barker's 17-year journey in aesthetics, focusing on personalized consultations, a comprehensive range of treatments, Flawless cuticles skincare, and integration of holistic wellness for optimal results.

BY BEN alan

In the ever-evolving landscape of aesthetics, one name stands out for its unwavering commitment to excellence and holistic care: Sarah Barker. As a seasoned practitioner with 17 years of experience in the field, Sarah's journey into aesthetics wasn't a predetermined path but rather a fortuitous encounter during her own quest for skin perfection. From that serendipitous moment, Sarah's passion for helping individuals achieve their aesthetic goals blossomed, leading her to become a Registered Nurse Prescriber and a trusted figure in the industry.

With over 10,000 treatments under her belt, Sarah's expertise extends far beyond the technicalities of procedures. She approaches each client interaction with a personalized touch, understanding that no two individuals are the same. Through comprehensive consultations and assessments, Sarah ensures that every client receives a tailored treatment plan that addresses their unique concerns and desires.

At Sarah's clinic, the range of treatments offered reflects her dedication to providing comprehensive care. From anti-wrinkle treatments to dermal fillers, medi-facials, and PDO threads, Sarah's arsenal is equipped to address a myriad of aesthetic needs. Yet, her commitment to skincare doesn't stop at the clinic doors. Recognizing the importance of at-home care, Sarah developed Flawlessceuticals, a cosmeceutical skincare line designed to complement and enhance the effects of in-clinic treatments.

However, Sarah's approach transcends mere physical enhancements. She understands the inseparable link between inner wellness and outer beauty, integrating skincare, and nutrition into her practice seamlessly. For Sarah, optimal results are not just about outward appearances but also about fostering overall well-being, both physical and mental.

In a world where the pursuit of beauty often neglects the essence of holistic care, Sarah Barker stands as a beacon of integrity and excellence. With her unwavering dedication to her clients' needs and well-being, she continues to redefine the standards of aesthetic practice, one personalized treatment at a time. Join us as we delve deeper into Sarah's insights, experiences, and the philosophy that drives her relentless pursuit of perfection in our exclusive interview with Entrepreneur Prime magazine.

Can you tell me about your experience in the aesthetics industry and what motivated you to become a Registered Nurse Prescriber?

Hi yes I have 17 years experience. I fell in to aesthetics by accident. I was having laser treatment for acne when I was looking for a job and the laser clinic wanted a nurse to work at the clinic doing the treatments and to train in botox and dermal fillers.

How do you approach consultations and assessments for your clients to ensure they receive personalized treatment plans tailored to their unique needs?

I meet and greet face to face, offer a drink and have an inormal chat. I then use a custom assessment template I designed myself using a face diagram and I get the clients to talk to me about what bothers them, while looking into a hand held mirror. I then tell them what and how we can improve things for them, educate them about the hows and why's I have come to the conclusions, check their medical history to make sure it is safe and right for them and then give them the template and report to take away and think about 'a cooling off period' before booking in for any treatments.

Could you elaborate on the range of treatments you offer at your clinic

A Journey into Personalised Care, Innovation, and Holistic Wellness

PHOTO: Sarah Barker epitomizes excellence in aesthetics, blending expertise, compassion, and innovation to redefine beauty standards and holistic care.

and how you stay updated with the latest advancements in aesthetic procedures?

I offer Anti wrinkle treatments, a variety of dermal fillers from fine, under eye, deep to volume. I do medi facials, skin care consultations. PDO threads and private medical diagnostic and prescribing for menopause etc.

I noticed you emphasize the importance of skincare in conjunction with aesthetic treatments. Can you share more about your Flawless Skin Boost and how it complements your procedures?

Hi I do, there is no point in my clients investing in in clinic treatments and not caring for and protecting their skin in between. I offer advice on what to use at home and also have a cosmeceutical/medical grade skincare range and collagen powder drink they can purchase to enable them to do this.

Your clinic seems to prioritise both the physical treatments and the holistic approach to skincare and nutrition. Could you provide insights into how you integrate these aspects to ensure optimal results for your clients?

Sure, as above, looking after the skin and wellbeing of my clients is my priority. As I am a nurse some clients will ask me about physical symptoms and mental health issues so I am glad I am prepared to help them as much as I can in all aspects of their lifestyle.

"

Janet
Hennessey
Dilenschneider
brings her unique
perspective to life,
creating serene
landscapes that
encourage a deeper
connection with the
environment.

PASCALE ROTHMAN
Redefines health with integrity, transparency, and innovation

By Lyra Green

In an era where wellness has become a buzzword, Pascale Rothman, the visionary Founder and CEO of More. Longevity & Wellbeing, stands at the forefront of a transformative movement. With a commitment to integrity, transparency, and community engagement, Rothman is redefining what it means to pursue health and well-being. In this exclusive feature with Beauty Prime magazine, she shares her insights on fostering a culture of innovation, addressing industry challenges, and the strategic vision that will guide More. Longevity & Wellbeing into the future. As the wellness landscape continues to evolve, Rothman's approach offers a refreshing perspective that prioritizes substance over trends, aiming to empower consumers to make informed choices for lasting health.

FOSTERING A CULTURE OF WELLNESS

At More. Longevity & Wellbeing, the commitment to fostering a culture of wellness is integral to operations. The company's ethos revolves around empowering its team members to share their expertise, creating an environment where everyone feels valued for their contributions. This foundation of mutual trust enhances job satisfaction, drives creativity, and encourages a sense of community. Rothman emphasizes that true innovation should never compromise integrity, a guiding principle that shapes the product development process. By prioritizing ethical practices and rigorous quality control, More. Longevity & Wellbeing ensures that its offerings consistently exceed consumer expectations.

Pascale Rothman, CEO of More. Longevity & Wellbeing, champions integrity, innovation, and transparency in wellness. Her vision prioritizes lasting health, empowering consumers with science-backed products and fostering meaningful community connections.

EMBRACING CHALLENGES AS OPPORTUNITIES

The wellness industry is currently facing significant challenges, particularly regarding product integrity. Many companies cut costs by providing ineffective dosages of ingredients, undermining product quality. Rothman views this

Pascale Rothman is a trailblazer in wellness, inspiring change with integrity, innovation, and a commitment to lasting health.

as an opportunity to elevate industry standards. More. Longevity & Wellbeing is committed to science and will not compromise on the essential elements of its products. The belief that wellness should be both achievable and a pleasurable experience sets the company apart in a highly saturated marketplace. By creating potent and palatable products, More. Longevity & Wellbeing enhances the consumer experience and promotes a genuine appreciation for nutrition. The organization is dedicated to the wellness journey, ensuring that its blends provide robust health advantages.

A VISION FOR LASTING HEALTH

Rothman's inspiration for leading More. Longevity & Wellbeing stems from a critical gap she identified in the wellness industry: the need for a brand that focuses on lasting health rather than fleeting fads. Many products promise quick fixes but overlook the principles of effective wellness. More. Longevity & Wellbeing advocates for a data-driven approach that emphasizes consistency, mindfulness, and the use of high-quality ingredients. The mission is to restore integrity and transparency in the Natural Products Industry, empowering consumers to make informed choices that enhance their wellness. By raising industry standards, the company seeks to deepen the connection between consumers and their health, reshaping the wellness landscape by prioritizing substance and efficacy.

STRATEGIC VISION FOR THE FUTURE

Looking ahead, Rothman has a well-defined strategic vision for More. Longevity & Wellbeing over the next five years. The organization aims to maintain its leadership position within the wellness industry by prioritizing transparency, efficacy, and quality. As the industry undergoes continual evolution, the company remains committed to its foundational principles, ensuring that its products are not only effective but also seamlessly integrated into daily routines. Plans for global expansion are underway, alongside a focus on innovation. Rothman envisions developing new products

that harmoniously combine natural potency with indulgent flavors—an aspect frequently neglected in the wellness sector.

INNOVATION AT THE CORE

Innovation is at the heart of More. Longevity & Wellbeing's product offerings. The company recognizes the demand for efficacious supplements, understanding that the success of such products relies on the quality, dosage, and synergy between the featured ingredients. The effectiveness of supplements begins with high-quality raw materials, and bioavailable compounds enhance absorption, making them more effective. Ingredients supported by scientific research are crucial for achieving desired outcomes, and the team is in tune with the latest trends and developments within the natural space.

MEASURING COMMUNITY IMPACT

Measuring impact on community health and wellness is another priority for More. Longevity & Wellbeing. The organization quantitatively assesses its success through the compelling narratives and transformative experiences shared by its community members. These individual accounts serve as evidence of the profound impact that the products provide. More. Longevity & Wellbeing prioritizes relationship-building over transactional sales. As the organization grows, there is a strategic intent to intensify these connections through direct community engagement and the establishment of educational platforms. By equipping consumers with knowledge and tools, the company aims to empower individuals who seek wellness.

A LASTING IMPACT

In a world where wellness trends often come and go, Pascale Rothman and More. Longevity & Wellbeing are committed to creating a lasting impact. By focusing on integrity, transparency, and community engagement, they are not just selling products; they are fostering a movement towards genuine well-being. As the wellness landscape continues to evolve, Rothman's vision and leadership will undoubtedly play a pivotal role in shaping the future of health and wellness for consumers everywhere.

How Heidi Ellert-McDermott Transformed Speechwriting with Innovation, Wit, and SpeechyAI

Heidi Ellert-McDermott's Speechy revolutionizes speechwriting, born from a need for witty wedding speeches. Overcoming SEO challenges, Speechy offers diverse services, led by top-notch writers. Marketing through PR and a book, Speechy aims to expand with SpeechyAI, balancing entrepreneurship with life challenges.

There are those that stand out not just for their innovation, but for their profound impact on personal moments and milestones. Enter Heidi Ellert-McDermott, a visionary entrepreneur who has reshaped the landscape of speechwriting with her brainchild, Speechy.

Heidi's journey into the realm of speechwriting was sparked by a cascade of wedding experiences where the speeches ranged from lackluster to cringe-worthy. Drawing from her background as a TV director and writer at the esteemed BBC, Heidi recognized an unmet need for modern, witty, and bespoke wedding speeches. Thus, Speechy was born.

What sets Speechy apart is not just its impeccable craftsmanship but also its adaptability. Evolving from its roots in wedding speeches, the company now offers a spectrum of services tailored to diverse needs and budgets. From speech edits to delivery coaching and even the groundbreaking SpeechyAI, Heidi's team ensures that every word resonates with authenticity and humor.

But the road to success was not without its challenges. Like any entrepreneur, Heidi faced the daunting task of navigating uncharted territory, from understanding SEO to mastering the art of delegation. Yet, fueled by her unwavering passion and commitment to excellence, she persevered, propelling Speechy to global acclaim.

What truly distinguishes Speechy is the caliber of its team. Comprised of industry luminaries who have graced the stages of BBC comedy shows and penned jokes for renowned comedians, Speechy's writers bring unparalleled expertise and warmth to every project. It's this winning combination of talent and empathy that has earned Speechy accolades from publications like The Observer and The New York Times.

As Heidi looks toward the future, her sights are set on further revolutionising the world of speechwriting with SpeechyAI. Powered by artificial intelligence and honed by the wisdom of Heidi's team, SpeechyAI promises to redefine how we craft speeches for weddings, businesses, and celebrations alike.

In the midst of her entrepreneurial journey, Heidi acknowledges the perpetual quest for balance between work and life, a challenge she tackles with characteristic grace and determination. Yet, through it all, her unwavering dedication to her craft and her clients remains steadfast, ensuring that every speech crafted by Speechy is not just memorable but truly unforgettable.

Join us as we delve into the remarkable story of Heidi Ellert-McDermott and the transformative power of Speechy, where every word is crafted with care and every moment is imbued with laughter and love.

How did you get the idea for your business and why did you think it would work?

In my early 30s I went to a succession of weddings where the speeches were variable to say the least. The brilliant ones added a wonderful moment to the day, but more often than not, the speeches were either awkward or dull. After sitting through a 40 min speech and seeing a trio of best men escorted away from the mic, I realised wedding speakers might appreciate the help for professional speechwriters.

Having worked in the TV industry, I had lots of contacts who I knew could work well with people and create truly unique and witty speeches for them. My team have worked on topical news quizzes and ghostwrite for renowned comedians, so wedding speakers now have access to truly great writers at a reasonable cost.

Over the years, we've developed our offering so in response to our clients varying needs, ability and budgets. We now also offer...

- A speech edit service (where clients send their first draft and we make it better)
- Delivery coaching (having directed TV presenters for over a decade, I know the dos and don't of presenting)
- Speech templates – (cheap, fast

turnaround option)

• SpeechyAI (combining our expertise with Artificial Intelligence)

What challenges did you find at the beginning of your journey and how did you overcome them?

Having never run my own business, I was completely ignorant about everything, other than the speechwriting and setting up a strong team!

The biggest learning curve has been understanding SEO as all our business is done online. We are a global business that offers both bespoke services and e-commerce products and we market to a wide variety of demographics (from best men in Australia wanting a bespoke speech, to a mother of the groom in the States wanting a simple speech template) so understanding our keywords and focussing our targeting has been key to our growth.

What makes your business unique?

Without a doubt, the quality of the Speechy team. They really are top of their game; writing for a range of BBC topical comedy shows, appearing in panel shows and ghostwriting for world-renowned comedians. They are also genuinely lovely people to work with and are excellent at building strong relationships with our clients.

What advice would you give to someone who is trying to become an entrepreneur?

It's not easy! Everything takes longer than you hope and costs a lot more too.

There's no silver bullet, and not much downtime in the initial years. There's lots of blood, sweat and tears and running your own business can be tough. But, as long as you know you're providing a great service or product, the effort feels worth it.

At Speechy as offer a delight guarantee because we want all our customers and clients to love working with us. I personally couldn't cope if they didn't! I care too much!

How did you market your business?

Because we offer such an unusual service and we have a lot of expertise, I've found it relatively easy to get good PR. We've been featured everywhere from The Telegraph to Forbes. I've also appeared on Radio 4's Women's Hour and BBC Sounds 'Best Men' podcast.

We don't pay for any editorial features; we simply supply interesting and entertaining content.

Due to our growing reputation as the go-to speech experts, the fantastic Little, Brown Publishers released my book, 'The Modern Couple's Guide to Wedding Speeches' last year. Great how-to book, and great publicity too!

What plans do you have for the future?

Our aim this year is to market SpeechyAI – https://www.speechy.com/product/speechyai/. We're confident it's a game-changer.

SpeechyAI utilises the power of Artificial Intelligence and the Speechy team's expertise to create wedding speeches that are funny, meaningful, and memorable. It's fun to use and affordable.

We'll be constantly improving it as the tech develops and we're also hoping to extend its ability beyond wedding speeches to business and celebration speeches too.

Exciting times ahead!

What's the biggest challenge of being an entrepreneur?

Having a work-life balance. (Still not quite mastered that one!)

Important to be able to delegate.

I've also learnt not to attempt all marketing routes, and instead concentrate on the few that have proven to work for us. It's impossible to master all marketing options – especially with so many social media channels, as well as PPC, mailing lists, SEO, and PR to consider.

Heidi Ellert-McDermott revolutionises speechwriting with Speechy, offering bespoke, witty speeches. From weddings to celebrations, her team, backed by SpeechyAI, crafts unforgettable moments with innovation and expertise.

SIMONA SPAN'S
STORMY NIGHT

"Embrace your uniqueness and step into the spotlight with Simona Span's signature 'Stormy Night' dress, where elegance meets empowerment. Join the journey of resilience and creativity, inspired by Romanian heritage, as passion becomes purpose."

Simona Span's Journey to Global Fashion Stardom

Empowering Women, Embracing Sustainability, and Redefining Style, One Stitch at a Timevolor sim expe conseque

Simona Span, founder of Simona Span Fashion, shares her journey from creating for her daughters to international acclaim. Her designs embrace sustainability, empower women, and envision innovative collaborations.

In the heart of Romania, amidst the serene landscapes of Negresti Oas, Simona Șpan, a proud mother of four, found her sanctuary and her calling. Her story is one of resilience, creativity, and an unwavering commitment to her dreams. From the quaint charm of her small town upbringing to the bustling runways of international fashion events, Simona's journey is nothing short of remarkable.

Amidst the challenges of the pandemic, Simona sought solace in the art of dressmaking, initially crafting garments for her daughters. Little did she know that this therapeutic endeavour would blossom into a flourishing fashion label, captivating hearts far beyond her hometown. Simona's creations, infused with love and inspired by her Romanian heritage, soon caught the eye of fashion enthusiasts worldwide.

In our exclusive interview with Simona Șpan for Entrepreneur Prime magazine, we delve into the intricacies of her ascent from a home-based hobbyist to a celebrated designer with a global presence. Her transition from sewing for her daughters to establishing her own fashion empire underscores the transformative power of passion and perseverance.

Simona's designs not only reflect her personal narrative but also resonate deeply with her clientele, embodying the spirit of empowerment and individuality. Her recent experience at the Pure London x JATC exhibition opened doors to new horizons, propelling her towards collaborations that bridge the worlds of fashion, art, and entertainment.

As sustainability takes centre stage in the fashion industry, Simona Șpan remains committed to ethical production practices. Her timeless creations, devoid of fleeting trends, embrace sustainability by prioritizing small-scale production and resource efficiency.

With each unique dress she creates, Simona Șpan champions the ethos of self-love and confidence, encouraging women to embrace their uniqueness with pride. Looking ahead, she envisions a future where technology and design converge to drive innovation while preserving precious resources.

Join us as we embark on a journey through Simona Șpan's world of fashion, where passion meets purpose, and dreams know no bounds.

What inspired you to transition from creating dresses for your daughters to establishing your own fashion label?

My biggest inspiration for expanding my brand, was the happiness of my clients. Whenever I was creating a dress for someone, the excitement in their eyes and the pure joy of wearing my designs, kept me going and motivated me to create more and more.

How do you believe your personal story and the beginnings of your brand resonate with your clientele?

I think lots of women out there resonate with my story. A single mother, trying her best, pushing the boundries, getting out of her confort zone just to be able to provide a good future for her daughters and following her passion! I would love to know that I'm a source of inspiration for women and show them that nothing is impossible and is never too late to follow your dream!

Could you share with us a highlight from your recent experience at the Pure London x JATC exhibition?

I had no idea what to expect from Pure London x JATC, but many people, after seeing my dresses on the catwalk, came to me and encouraged me to expand my work and my vision towards movie, cinema and theatre world, combining my work with art like opera, exhibitions of painting and other exclusivist events.

How does your Romanian heritage influence your designs, and how are you integrating this into the global fashion scene?

My designs are influenced by the places I've grew up in. I love colours, I love nature, the floral prints, the landscapes from my hometown were my biggest source of inspiration.

What challenges have you faced in scaling your brand from a local business to an international one, and how have you overcome them?

Actually I cannot talk about a local business, because after my first appereance in Romania, almost every invitation that followed was international: Italy, Canada, Dubai, France, England, America. In some we were able to go, but some of them are on our pending list, looking forward to go this year.

Sustainability is a significant conversation in fashion today. How does Simona Șpan address sustainability in its production processes?

Thanks to the fact that our dresses are timeless, so they don't follow trends, sustainability inside our company translates into limiting production to small series, without unnecessary merchandise stocks and avoiding the consumption of resources until they are clearly dedicated to a targeted consumption.

What is the philosophy behind the unique dresses you create, and how do you want women to feel when wearing your designs?

The philosophy behind my designs is that every woman is unique and special. Every woman should embrace this uniqueness and love everything about her, feel empowered, have confidence and be brave enough to wear something that is created just for her!

Looking towards the future, what direction do you see Simona Șpan taking, and are there any upcoming projects or collaborations we can look forward to?

Now we work at a new project that will combine new technology with design, specially developed to save resources such as fabrics, time, production costs. This project comes to help the production efficiency and implementing sustainability too.

Introducing
KATIE LYNCH
Crafting Magic in Every Event

Embarking on a journey of creativity and celebration, Katie Lynch, the visionary CEO and Director of Katie J Design and Events, invites us into her world of magic and innovation. With a passion for transforming ordinary spaces into extraordinary experiences, Katie's story unfolds with the flicker of inspiration ignited during her tenure at Warner Bros Movie World.

Immersed in the glitz and glamour of premieres for iconic films like Cats & Dogs and Harry Potter, Katie found herself enchanted by the meticulous artistry of event planning and design. From those star-studded beginnings, her path led her through academic achievements and professional milestones, culminating in the birth of Katie J Design and Events in 2014.

But Katie's journey isn't just about crafting beautiful events; it's about infusing each celebration with the essence of her clients' dreams. From weddings dripping with romance to corporate gatherings pulsating with professionalism, Katie's bespoke approach ensures that no two events are ever the same.

At the heart of Katie's work lies a commitment to sustainability and eco-conscious practices.

Katie Lynch's innovative approach to event planning captivates, inspiring magic and sustainability. A visionary in her field, she transforms dreams into reality.

Beyond the glitz and glam, she champions initiatives that minimize environmental impact, ensuring that every event leaves a positive imprint on the world.

In a realm where trends flicker like stars in the night sky, Katie's designs stand as timeless beacons of elegance and innovation. Seamlessly blending the latest trends

Katie Lynch, CEO of Katie J Design and Events, shares her journey from Warner Bros to eco-friendly event planning, blending creativity and sustainability.

with classic sophistication, she crafts experiences that transcend fleeting fashions, leaving an indelible mark on every guest's memory.

But perhaps what truly sets Katie apart is her unwavering spirit of adaptability and resilience. Like a true magician, she turns challenges into opportunities, transforming setbacks into moments of brilliance that illuminate her path forward.

As we step into the world of Katie J Design and Events, we're invited to dream, to create, and to celebrate. From magical beginnings to sustainable futures, Katie Lynch reminds us that the true magic of any event lies in the joy it brings and the memories it creates. So let's raise our glasses and toast to the enchanting journey ahead, guided by the visionary spirit of Katie Lynch.

Could you tell us about the inspiration behind starting Katie J Design and Events? What motivated you to venture into event planning and design?

My journey into event planning and design was sparked by a lifelong love for decorating and celebrating. It all began during my time at Warner Bros Movie World, where I had the opportunity to work on some truly spectacular events like premieres for Cats & Dogs, Harry Potter, and Scooby-Doo. From setting up themed banquets to being backstage for star-studded concerts, I was captivated by the meticulous attention

to detail that went into transforming spaces into thematic wonderlands. These experiences fuelled my desire to delve deeper into the realm of event management.

After completing my traineeship, I pursued a Double Diploma in Events and Hospitality Management, graduating with distinctions and credits. Subsequently, I immersed myself in the role of Functions Coordinator at the Jindalee Entertainment Venue, orchestrating a diverse array of events ranging from weddings and birthdays to conferences and concerts. But as life took me down the path of parenthood, I found myself yearning for a way to blend my love for events with the joys of family life.

That's when inspiration struck - quite literally at my own children's birthday parties! With each passing year, I found myself crafting more elaborate themes and decorations, much to the delight of family and friends. Their encouragement gave me the push I needed to turn my passion into a profession, and thus, Katie J Design and Events was born in 2014. My mission? To sprinkle a little magic into the lives of others by creating custom-themed decorations for their special celebrations.

Your website showcases a wide range of events, from weddings to corporate gatherings. How do you approach tailoring your design and planning services to meet the unique needs of each client and event type?

At Katie J Design and Events, we're all about making dreams come true, one event at a time. That's why we've teamed up with Customily to take customisation to a whole new level. Now, our clients have the power to personalise their event decorations like never before! Whether it's tweaking colors, adding special messages, or choosing their favourite font, the possibilities are endless. From weddings that sparkle with romance to corporate gatherings that exude professionalism, we've got something for everyone.

We believe that the best events are the ones where clients' visions shine through. Our online editor allows clients to preview their customisations in real-time, providing them with unparalleled creative control over their event décor. With an extensive range of products available for customisation, including invitations, banners, and stickers, clients can seamlessly tailor their decorations to suit their unique preferences. After all, it's your event - why not make it as unique as you are?

Customisation seems to be a key aspect of your work, as mentioned on your website. Could you elaborate on how you collaborate with clients to bring their vision to life while also infusing your expertise and creativity into the process?

With over 400 themes and designs to choose from in our online store, the possibilities are endless. But if there's one thing we've learned, it's that sometimes, the perfect theme is one that hasn't been created yet. That's where our 'Create your Own' party decorations range fills the void. Clients can upload their own special photo or image, add their own text, or even an entire design that they have created from scratch using software like Canva.

Our online editor guides clients

"

EVENT MAESTRO

Katie Lynch – Winner "Best National Kids Party Stylist/Planner" at the What's on 4 Kids Awards 2023-24 CEO and Director of Katie J Design and Events

effortlessly through the creation of their custom décor, while our dedicated Customer Service team is available to provide assistance and support during business hours. We are committed to assisting clients in crafting unique party decorations with our premium quality products. With our online editor, clients can easily visualise their ideas in real-time, ensuring that every detail meets their expectations.

Sustainability and eco-friendliness are increasingly important considerations for many clients. How does Katie J Design and Events incorporate sustainable practices into event planning and design?

Sustainability isn't just a trend for us - it's a way of life. That's why we're committed to minimising our environmental footprint in everything we do. From using eco-friendly materials where possible to reducing waste in our production process, we're always looking for ways to do better. And as a mum of three, I know how important it is to leave the world a little better than we found it.

That's why we're proud to donate any leftover materials to local schools and kindergartens for arts and crafts projects. And as we look to the future, we're exploring even more ways to make a positive impact, from recycling plastics to reducing our energy consumption. Because when it comes to sustainability, every little bit helps.

In the world of event planning and design, trends evolve rapidly. How do you stay current with industry trends while also ensuring that your designs have a timeless quality?

In an industry where trends evolve rapidly, staying current is essential. At Katie J Design and Events, we

pride ourselves on our ability to anticipate and adapt to changing trends while maintaining a timeless quality in our designs. Each new design/theme undergoes thorough research and analysis to ensure that it resonates with current market trends.

That's why our creations are as timeless as they are trendy. Whether you're looking for a classic wedding theme or a modern corporate look, we've got you covered. And with our versatile designs, you can rest assured knowing that your event will stand the test of time.

Can you share a particularly memorable or challenging event that you've worked on? How did you overcome any obstacles, and what lessons did you learn from that experience?

Every event has its challenges, but it's how we overcome them that defines us. Take my daughter's Mermaid-themed birthday party, for example. With two weeks of non-stop rain leading up to the big day, I knew we'd have to get creative. Drawing inspiration from the theme itself, I transformed our outdoor area into an underwater wonderland using tarps and decorations.

What initially seemed like a setback turned into an opportunity for innovation, as the makeshift setup added an unexpected charm to the event. This experience taught me the importance of adaptability and creative problem-solving, skills that continue to serve me well in my career. So there you have it - a little glimpse into the world of Katie J Design and Events. From magical beginnings to sustainable futures, we're here to make your dreams come true, one event at a time. Let's create an amazing celebration together!

PHOTO: Melinda Nicci, CEO and Founder of Baby2Body, Championing Women's Wellness with Passion and Purpose."

A Conversation with

MELINDA NICCI

Empowers Women Through Wellness

Embodying a holistic approach to women's wellness, Melinda Nicci stands as a beacon of innovation and advocacy. With a rich tapestry of qualifications including Sport Psychologist, fitness trainer, and best-selling author, Nicci's journey culminates in her role as CEO and Founder of Baby2Body—a pivotal member of the Body Collective family of women's health apps. For over three decades, she has championed the cause of women's wellness, continually pushing boundaries to redefine the standards of holistic health. Since the inception of the Baby2Body app in 2018, Nicci's digital platforms have nurtured over 5 million women worldwide, offering tailored solutions to every stage of the female journey.

Melinda Nicci discusses founding Baby2Body to bridge fitness gaps for women. She blends sports psychology insights with AI for personalised wellness, empowering millions worldwide.

Drawing from her diverse expertise, Nicci sheds light on the genesis of Baby2Body and the profound impact of her background in Sports Psychology on the platform's ethos. "I came up with the idea for Baby2Body after having my first child," she shares, emphasizing the stark void she perceived in the fitness landscape concerning pre- and postnatal care. Fuelled by a vision of inclusivity and scalability, Nicci embarked on a transformative journey, blending her insights from sports psychology with a mastery of consumer healthcare innovation to birth the groundbreaking Baby2Body app.

Looking towards the horizon, Nicci envisions a future where Baby2Body serves as a bastion of personalized wellness, leveraging AI to craft bespoke experiences for every user. The recent introduction of Bella, an AI wellness coach integrated within the Baby2Body ecosystem, heralds a new era of tailored support for women worldwide. "Our vision for Baby2Body's future revolves around enhancing personalization in health and wellness," Nicci asserts, underscoring the platform's unwavering commitment to women's empowerment.

Central to Baby2Body's ethos is the comprehensive suite of resources it offers to support pregnant women on their transformative journey. From personalized fitness programs to evidence-based nutritional guidance and round-the-clock access to expert advice through Bella, the platform serves as a steadfast companion, empowering women with knowledge, tools, and unwavering support.

A cornerstone of Baby2Body's success lies in its collaboration with a diverse cadre of experts. Registered dietitians, certified personal trainers, and wellness coaches converge to curate content that is not only accurate and evidence-based but also deeply empathetic to the needs of its audience. "We take pride in collaborating with a diverse team of experts," Nicci emphasizes, underlining the platform's commitment to excellence in women's health.

As guardians of accuracy and integrity, Baby2Body meticulously curates its content, drawing from reputable sources and subjecting every piece to rigorous scrutiny. With a trust score of 92%, the platform stands as a paragon of reliability in the realm of women's wellness, continuously evolving to reflect the latest advancements in prenatal and postnatal care.

In the dynamic landscape of women's wellness, Melinda Nicci and Baby2Body emerge as trailblazers, offering a beacon of hope and empowerment to millions of women worldwide. As they continue to innovate and evolve, their commitment to holistic health and unwavering support for women at every stage of life remains resolute.

What inspired you to create Baby2Body and how has your background as a Sports Psychologist influenced the platform?

I came up with the idea for Baby2Body after having my first child, recognizing a glaring gap in the fitness industry for pre- and postnatal needs. Determined to bridge this void, I established a boutique fitness company offering personal training tailored to pregnancy and postpartum. I saw the potential for scalability, so I pursued a Master's in Sports Psychology and gained valuable insights from spending a few years as a Senior Director in consumer healthcare innovation at Philips. These experiences culminated in the launch of the Baby2Body app in 2018. Since then, we've reached over 5 million women across 125 countries, becoming the leading prenatal wellness app. Our platform offers personalized wellness experiences rooted in evidence-based practices encompassing nutrition, fitness, and emotional wellbeing, all supported by behavior change concepts and how to achieve optimal performance rooted in Sports Psychology.

How do you see Baby2Body evolving in the future to further support women's wellness and empowerment?

Our vision for Baby2Body's future revolves around enhancing personalization in health and wellness, leveraging AI to achieve this goal. We recently developed and launched Bella, the pioneering AI women's wellness coach exclusively available within the Baby2Body app, so we're already advancing in this direction. Bella is trained extensively on our content and user data, enabling women to access personalized insights and guidance tailored to their unique wellness journey during motherhood. We're leveraging Bella not only to offer personalized recommendations but also to integrate product suggestions aimed at promoting women's thriving health.

What resources do you provide on your app to support pregnant women in their journey?

Baby2Body offers a one-stop shop for women at any stage in their motherhood journey. We offer a comprehensive range of resources specifically designed to support the mother's health, these resources include:

• Personalized Fitness Programs: Tailored exercise routines suitable for each stage of pregnancy, ensuring safe and effective workouts.

• Nutrition Guidance: Evidence-based nutritional advice and meal plans to support the nutritional needs of both mother and baby during pregnancy.

• Wellness Tips: Expert tips and articles covering various aspects of pregnancy wellness, including emotional wellbeing, stress management, and sleep optimization.

• Health Tracking: Tools to monitor and track pregnancy milestones, appointments, and symptoms, providing valuable insights into overall health and wellbeing.

• AI Wellness Coach: Direct access to Bella, offering 24/7 and instant chat support based on the wealth of knowledge from our team of experts, including nutritionists, fitness trainers, and healthcare professionals, for personalized guidance and support.

By providing these resources, we aim to empower pregnant women with the knowledge, tools, and support they need to navigate motherhood.

Can you tell me more about the experts and professionals involved in creating the content on your platform?

We take pride in collaborating with a diverse team of experts to create high-quality and evidence-based content for our platform – and they can all be found on our website! They include:

• Registered dietitians who develop guidance on prenatal and postnatal nutrition, meal planning, and healthy eating habits

• Certified personal trainers and fitness experts who develop safe and effective workout programs

• Certified wellness coaches and mental health experts who specialize in holistic approaches to women's health, offering advice on lifestyle changes, stress management, and self-care practices.

We don't provide any direct medical guidance, but we have worked with healthcare professionals and organizations in the development of our content to ensure its accuracy and alignment with best practices for prenatal and postnatal care.

How do you ensure the information provided on your website is accurate and up-to-date for expecting mothers? 6. How do you ensure that the information provided on women's health is evidence-based and trustworthy for your audience?

The accuracy and integrity of our content is of the utmost importance to us, and that's reflected in how our community feels about our content (we have a trust score of 92%). All content is created by qualified wellness experts and/or sourced from esteemed publications such as peer-reviewed journals, medical associations, and government health agencies. Additionally, we rigorously fact-check what we put out and continuously monitor new research, guidelines, and advancements in prenatal and postnatal health, promptly updating our content as needed to reflect the latest developments.

"
WHISPERING SECRETS

Melinda Nicci pioneers holistic women's wellness, merging expertise in sports psychology with digital innovation, positively impacting millions globally

Unveiling Insights with

SHERRY ARGOV

Decoding Relationships, Empowering Women, and Redefining Love

Sherry Argov, the acclaimed author of Why Men Marry Bitches and Why Men Love Bitches, has captivated readers worldwide with her insightful take on relationships. Renowned as "America's Top Relationship Guide" by Book Tribe and hailed as one of the "Ten Most Iconic Books of the Past Decade" by Yahoo, Argov's influence extends far beyond the pages of her bestselling books.

With over 100 magazine features and appearances on national television shows like The Today Show and The View, Sherry Argov has become a household name in the realm of romance and self-empowerment. Her message resonates deeply with readers, challenging common misconceptions about love and urging women to embrace their independence and self-worth.

In this exclusive interview with Entrepreneur Prime Magazine, Sherry Argov delves into the inspiration behind her books, sharing insights gained from interviews with hundreds of men and offering practical advice for navigating the complexities of modern relationships. From debunking myths about romance to empowering women to stand up for themselves, Argov's wisdom shines through as she encourages readers to prioritize their own happiness and fulfilment.

As her bestselling books continue to soar to the top of international bestseller lists and inspire readers of all ages and backgrounds, Sherry Argov's universal message of self-confidence and empowerment transcends cultural boundaries. With each page turn, readers discover the transformative power of embracing their true selves and asserting their worth in every aspect of life.

Join us as we delve into the mind of this influential author and relationship expert, and uncover the keys to building healthier, more fulfilling partnerships in a world where love and self-respect reign supreme.

Your books, *Why Men Love Bitches* and *Why Men Marry Bitches*, have been acclaimed as insightful relationship guides garnering significant attention and praise. What inspired you to write these books, and what do you hope readers will take away from them?

Thank you for your kind words, which are very gracious. My inspiration came from the insightful feedback that I received from many men I interviewed who shared what they secretly respect and desire in a woman. It was very surprising to me to learn that the traits men want are the opposite of what most women believe. Most women believe they will be valued more if they try harder and do more to please their boyfriends or husbands. In my interviews with men, they explained that they do not want a woman who consistently sacrifices herself and who puts him on a pedestal. Instead, men desire and respect a woman who is more self-assured, independent and confident in herself, and less needy of reassurance from him. The message of my books is to always keep your

Why Men Love Bitches by Sherry Argov explores why men are drawn to strong, self-assured women. Packed with witty insights and practical advice, it empowers women to command respect while maintaining romantic allure.

life, maintain your independence and to pursue other interests outside of your relationship. My message to women is to always stand on your own two feet. Your happiness should not depend on another person.

Both of your books delve into the dynamics of romantic relationships and offer practical advice for women seeking to assert themselves and navigate the dating world more confidently. What are some common misconceptions about relationships that you address through your writing?

Let's start with the misconception that if you are all-giving, overly generous and always available, you will get the same in return. Most women have given too much of themselves in a relationship and relate to the feeling of being taken for granted. My books explain why giving too much to someone (especially someone you've just met) may backfire, and why it doesn't always

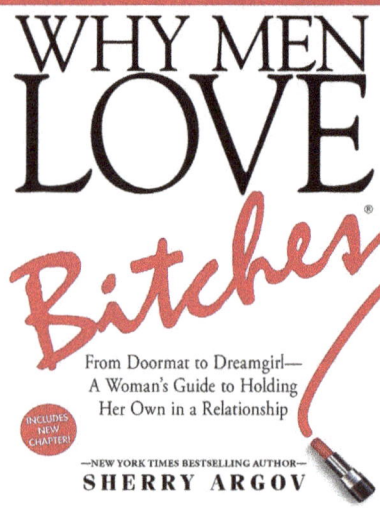

lead to the desired response from your partner in return. Successful relationships take time and people tend to value what they've earned. My books give specific examples that lead to a more balanced and successful relationship.

Another misconception is that a woman's beauty will lead to success in relationships. Most women are led to believe that if she is beautiful, a man will appear on a white horse, pay all her bills and solve all her problems. Yet beautiful women can have terrible relationships, while ordinary women are treated like queens. The men I interviewed desire a woman who has her own values, principles, goals, and a strong sense of who she is. They also shared that it's rare to find a woman who believes in herself. This is not just my opinion. It's what men told me over and over. A confident woman is never ordinary.

In Why Men Love Bitches, and Why Men Marry Bitches you emphasize the importance of women standing up for themselves and maintaining their independence in relationships. Can you elaborate on

Why Men Marry Bitches: THE EXPANDED NEW EDITION is a game-changer! With humour and sisterly advice, Argov decodes the mysteries of relationships, empowering readers to embrace confidence and win the love they deserve. A must-read!

WHY MEN MARRY

Bitches

A Guide for Women Who Are *Too* Nice

INCLUDES TWO NEW CHAPTERS!

—NEW YORK TIMES BESTSELLING AUTHOR—
SHERRY ARGOV

why you believe these qualities are attractive to men, and how they contribute to healthier and more fulfilling partnerships?

Men like a challenge, and they want an equal partner. When a woman has a dynamic, interesting life, men want to be a part of it. It draws them in. Most men will be more appreciative that a woman who has to make time for him and they tend to work harder to become a part of that woman's life. When I talk about being a "challenge" I'm not only referring to how quickly a relationship is consummated in the bedroom. A woman who is a "challenge" doesn't move a man to the top of her priority list within the first week and pick up the phone on the first ring. She doesn't text multiple times a day. If she is interested in her own life, it shows. When a woman has goals, activities, interests and a fuller life outside of a relationship, and she isn't available all the time, most men will respect her time and attention much more.

Your work has been featured in numerous magazines worldwide and you have made appearances on national television. How do you feel about the widespread impact and recognition of your books, particularly in influencing discussions about relationships?

It is fulfilling to know that I have helped women and that I can earn a living doing something I enjoy. With regard to public recognition, it's a two-edged sword. Being in the public eye exposes you to people voicing their opinions online anonymously, and you don't always see the best side of human nature on the internet when they can hide behind a fake name. However, every day I am inspired by the many women who were helped by my books, and who feel much more confident and empowered after reading them. I enjoy hearing all the success stories from my readers.

Your books have been translated into over thirty languages and continue to be bestsellers worldwide. What do you think contributes to the universal appeal and relevance of your insights on relationships across different cultures and societies?

People from different countries may speak different languages, and eat different foods. But all human beings want love, dignity and respect. The emails that I receive from a woman in Europe will usually express the same feelings, insecurities, concerns and hopes as an email that I receive from a woman in India, or Latin America. Thank goodness for Google translate. The people who read my books are also very diverse in age. My audience includes men and women including pre-teens, college aged-women, middle-aged people, mothers, fathers, and senior citizens who are re-entering the dating scene late in life. I find it fascinating to see how similar we all are particularly in romantic relationships. If you're a woman reading this and you are struggling with something, you are not alone.

As a bestselling author and relationship expert, what advice would you give to women who may be struggling to find their voice or assert themselves in their relationships? Are there any key principles or strategies from your books that you believe are particularly important for women to embrace in their romantic lives?

When you begin to assert yourself, be clear, be respectful and speak your mind. Say what you mean and mean what you say. But don't say it meanly. It's never mean to let a man hear you speak your truth and see you stand up for yourself. When you believe in yourself, your partner will believe in you more as well. He will respect you more when you show respect for yourself. It's important to remember that a man should never be the reason you are happy. He should add to your happiness. Remind yourself daily that you are worthy and you deserve to be happy. It's a mindset. Choose your dignity and peace of mind over impressing others. Once you start to believe in yourself, things start to change for the better. Confidence is a superpower.

"Sherry Argov's profound insights and empowering message redefine love, inspiring women worldwide to embrace confidence, independence, and self-worth."

PHOTO: *Capturing Moments: A Father's Loving Gaze and a Son's Curious Glance - Family Joy in Every Frame."*

Empowers Wellness
DR. KRISTIAN EDWARDS

The Future of Wellness: Dr. Edwards' Vision for BLK + GRN and Beyond

In the realm of wellness and conscious living, Dr. Kristian Edwards stands as a beacon of empowerment and change. As a professor of public health and a fervent advocate for natural lifestyle choices, she embodies the essence of holistic well-being. However, it's her role as the visionary behind BLK + GRN that truly underscores her commitment to fostering healthier, happier communities.

BLK + GRN isn't just a marketplace; it's a testament to Dr. Edwards' unwavering belief in the power of #BlackGirlMagic and the transformative potential of mindful consumerism. Conceived as an avenue to support Black artisans while promoting toxin-free living, BLK + GRN offers a curated

"Dr. Kristian Edwards discusses founding BLK + GRN to offer toxin-free products from Black artisans, fostering holistic wellness and community empowerment.

selection of all-natural products spanning skincare, home essentials, and bath and body care. It's a testament to Dr. Edwards' dedication to providing a platform where individuals can align their purchasing decisions with their values, supporting both personal health and economic empowerment within the Black community.

The genesis of BLK + GRN finds its roots in a deeply personal journey. Motivated by a desire to mitigate the disparities highlighted in the Environmental Working Group's research, Dr. Edwards embarked on a quest to embrace natural, non-toxic products. Her quest led her to realize the intersectionality of her mission—to not only prioritize personal wellness but also uplift Black-owned businesses.

Central to BLK + GRN's ethos is the meticulous curation of its offerings. Dr. Edwards and her team employ a rigorous selection process, ensuring that each product meets stringent criteria for quality, safety, and alignment with the platform's values.

Through this approach, BLK + GRN has emerged as a trusted destination for those seeking products that not only nurture the body but also reflect a commitment to sustainability and community well-being.

Yet, Dr. Edwards' vision extends beyond commerce. It's about fostering a dialogue, empowering individuals to make informed choices, and cultivating a culture of holistic wellness. Through initiatives like her engagement on social media platforms, she seeks to inspire and educate, bridging the gap between consumer and creator.

As BLK + GRN continues to flourish, Dr. Edwards remains steadfast in her dedication to amplifying Black voices, championing natural living, and nurturing a community of empowered individuals. Her vision for the future is one of growth, innovation, and continued advocacy—a vision where wellness is not just a lifestyle but a catalyst for positive change.

In conversation with Entrepreneur

Prime Magazine, Dr. Kristian Edwards shares insights into the genesis of BLK + GRN, its commitment to quality and community, and the transformative power of conscious consumerism. Join us as we delve into the heart of a movement that's redefining wellness, one product at a time.

What inspired the creation of BLK + GRN, and how do you ensure that the products featured on your platform align with your mission of promoting natural and healthy living?

I read, "Study: Women of Colour Exposed to More Toxic Chemicals in Personal Care Products" in 2017 by the Environmental Working Group. It showed how products marketed to Black people are more toxic than products marketed to every other demographic. I was personally committed to using products that were natural and non-toxic. On this journey, I read the book Our Black Year, which discussed how individuals had a lot of power to uplift Black businesses if they purchased their products. So I modified my list to be natural products by Black-owned companies. However, I had to go to a lot of websites to order the products I wanted and I had to test them for effectiveness. I created BLK + GRN to be an easy one-stop shop to find non-toxic and Black owned products.

My mission has and always will be to connect Black women to the tools, resources, knowledge, and products they need to lead happier and healthier lives. I believe that a life free of toxins and all things artificial is a life worth cultivating. My purpose through BLK + GRN is to help Black women do exactly that while also elevating and incubating a group of Black women artisans who otherwise would not have a place to share their stories or their products with the very people they created them for. Since 2017, BLK + GRN has elevated over 100 Black-owned brands and shipped over 18,500 orders of non-toxic products placed on our marketplace.

How do you select the Black artisans and creators featured on BLK + GRN, and what criteria must their products meet before being included in your marketplace?

At BLK + GRN, our all Black artisans are carefully chosen by Black women's health experts who know what an all-natural product truly looks like. We've seen first-hand the damaging effects harmful ingredients and practices have had on our community. Our marketplace connects Black women with natural lifestyles to high-quality, toxic-free brands that share in our mission of health, wellness and community cultivation. We promise to maintain that connection by curating, crafting and consuming consciously for you. We use a 4 step onboarding process:

1. Discover - We love finding small Black artisan brands that are high quality and really meeting a unique need. We have hundreds of artisans that we have discovered, but we are not interested in carrying every product possible; we curate our selection to include only the best of the best of Black-owned brands.

2. Alignment - We only partner with Artisans that have built their brands on the values at the heart of BLK + GRN — health, wellness, and community cultivation. We go deeper with the Artisan, asking questions about sourcing, packaging, personality, and community responsibility.

3. Quality Assurance - We wouldn't bring anything that's toxic into our home, or yours. We check each product ingredient against our Toxic Twenty List- which was developed utilizing

the latest research - and we ensure that nothing scores above a 5 for toxicity. We want to be absolutely sure we're offering you the cleanest plant-based products on the market.

4. Test - Once we've ensured safety, we test for effectiveness. For this, we turn to aestheticians, dermatologists, makeup artists and other professionals to use the product and report back on effectiveness and quality. Dr. Kristian personally tests every single product!

What measures does BLK + GRN take to ensure product quality and customer satisfaction, and how do you handle feedback and returns?

BLK + GRN aims for 100% customer satisfaction. While all sales are final and we do not accept returns, we want to hear from you if you are not happy with your purchase. If our customer receives a damaged or incorrect order, we ship them a replacement. If they have feedback on the product itself we share it with the creator to incorporate in their constant analysis of their product.

As a marketplace focused on natural and non-toxic products, how does BLK + GRN stay updated on industry trends and regulations to maintain the integrity of your offerings?

We use the Environment Working Group's (EWG) Skin Deep® database to stay up to date on the research around the toxicity of ingredients in personal care products. When we discuss ingredient safety in our ingredient library, we regularly refer to the EWG's safety and sustainability rating because we consider their data fairly reliable, and their research is public. Their scoring system is between 1-10 when rating ingredient safety and sustainability.

Looking towards the future, how do you envision the growth of BLK + GRN, and are there any upcoming initiatives or partnerships that you're particularly excited about?

I am really excited about my TikTok and going live more on IG. I am getting emails from my customers that they want more information from me about healthy living. I am so excited to talk about healthy eating, easily incorporating exercise into daily activities, self-love tips, gardening, in addition to my use of non-toxic products.

"
EMPOWERS WELLNESS

Dr. Kristian Edwards embodies empowerment, leading BLK + GRN with unwavering dedication to health, community, and conscious consumerism

PHOTO:*Jacqueline Iversen, Co-Founder and Chief Clinical Officer of Sen-Jam Pharmaceutical, leading the charge in innovative and proactive pain management solutions.*

Wisdom from a Wellness Innovator
JACQUELINE IVERSEN
Empowering Future Pharmacists and Entrepreneurs

Jacqueline Iversen discusses Sen-Jam Pharmaceutical's innovative approach to pain management, emphasizing proactive solutions, accessibility, and the importance of creativity and perseverance in healthcare.

When it comes to innovation in pain management and wellness, few names resonate as strongly as Jacqueline Iversen. As the Co-Founder and Chief Clinical Officer of Sen-Jam Pharmaceutical, Jackie has dedicated her career to rethinking the traditional paradigms of the pharmaceutical industry. Her extensive background in pharmacokinetics and pain management, combined with her unwavering commitment to improving patient outcomes, has positioned her as a visionary in the field. With over two decades of scientific contributions, including more than 20 published papers, Jackie is not only a leader in clinical research but also a passionate advocate for proactive and preventive healthcare solutions.

Jackie's journey began with a vision during her research fellowship at Memorial Sloan Kettering, where she recognized the need for a shift from reactive to proactive pain management strategies. Her expertise as a hospital pharmacist, coupled with her deep understanding of the challenges faced by patients, inspired her to co-found Sen-Jam Pharmaceutical alongside her husband, Jim, a logistics and efficiency expert. Together, they have cultivated a unique approach to drug development, focusing on low-cost, repurposed therapeutics that aim to reduce healthcare expenditures while expanding access to underserved populations.

In this exclusive interview for Entrepreneur Prime Magazine, Jackie shares her insights on the inspiration behind Sen-Jam Pharmaceutical, the personal experiences that fuel her determination to address inflammation, pain, and addiction, and the innovative strategies her company employs to navigate the complexities of the pharmaceutical industry. She also provides valuable advice for aspiring pharmacists and entrepreneurs, emphasizing the importance of creativity, perseverance, and data-driven decision-making in driving meaningful change.

Join us as we delve into the mind of a true wellness innovator and explore the future of pain management and global health through the eyes of Jacqueline Iversen.

How did you and your husband Jim come up with the idea to start Sen-Jam Pharmaceutical?

I founded Sen-Jam Pharmaceutical because I had a vision around improving our current standard of both wanted that challenge.

What personal experiences have shaped your determination to create solutions for inflammation, pain, and addiction?

As a pharmacist, but more so, as a human, seeing the devastation and suffering brought onto individuals and their families, plaguing our society and the world by unethical pharmaceutical business practices, utilizing addictive drugs, makes me so angry, that I have felt a personal duty to use my knowledge to help out where I can. I realized, had alternative pharmaceutical products been developed just before Oxycontin, we could have reduced the risk and devastation of widespread opioid addiction and dependence. I believe that drug development has the potential to change prescribing and drug policy, by educating everyone, and I wanted to share my knowledge this way. An idea that could be distributed to many. That's where my research began, treating pain with a non-opioid agent that also reduces the harmful effects of opioids. And along the way, I've additionally discovered new treatments to reduce inflammation, and safely modulate the immune system, which coincidentally, is intimately tied to pain and addiction.

What challenges have you faced in developing low-cost therapeutics for underserved populations, and how have you overcome them?

The majority of drugs, over 50% each year that obtain FDA approval, are repurposed, low-cost therapeutics that could reduce healthcare expenditure - particularly in the United States, but elsewhere as well - and expand access to all populations. And the majority of companies develop drugs in that repurposed space; which makes it very crowded. Yet, the larger investors focus on what we would consider "designer drugs" which are where larger pharma companies reside. That risk to reward benefit is extremely high. This designer investment

Jacqueline Iversen is a pioneering force in clinical pain management and pharmaceutical innovation, dedicated to transforming patient care and advancing wellness.

pain management which stemmed from my research fellowship at Memorial Sloan Kettering in New York City. It was during that time, decades ago, that I first became fascinated by how the medical community treated pain well after the fact or reactively instead of considering means of preventing or mitigating it proactively. I am a hospital pharmacist who loves science and sees thousands of people yearly who continue to struggle with ailments, despite the plethora of medications currently available. I have always wanted to improve outcomes with evidence based ideas that challenge the status quo. As for my husband; he's a brilliant business mind rooted deeply in logistics and efficiency. Bringing that sharp solutions-orientation to the infamously old-school pharma industry has been a true competitive advantage to our success. Rethinking the industry paradigm, with Jim at the helm as CEO and I as Chief Clinical Officer, we believed it would result in new, more innovative products reaching patients in need. And we

model makes the length of time to develop a drug longer, for both the pharmaceutical company and the patient. Which is where Sen-Jam sees the opportunity of rapidly and at low cost, developing innovative products that can challenge the larger pharmaceutical company inventions by targeting the same unique mechanism of action, but with an already available, known to be safe, drug. So being nimble, is our secret sauce, as we leverage new technology (i.e. artificial intelligence, digital clinical trials, companion diagnostics, collaborative partnerships, etc.) to achieve our goals of bringing new and superior solutions to patients as fast as possible.

How do you envision the future of Sen-Jam Pharmaceutical in terms of its impact on global health?

Sen-Jam is on a mission to extend healthy aging by safely modulating our immune system. The immune system is just now, being understood and mapped, into a vast web of differentiated cells and mediators that influence our health for a lifetime. Sen-Jam's mission is to support an individual's immune system, by first ensuring propering monitoring, and measuring of the immune system's role in health and disease. And secondly, or more deliberately, treating inflammation further upstream proactively (meaning before tissue damage and disease have taken root) than current therapeutics do. It's currently believed that with overuse, our immune system can become fragile, and slow, leading to diseases that require very potent, immunosuppressive treatments (i.e. costly "designer drugs" for Inflammatory bowel disease, arthritis, cancer, etc). By targeting inflammation using a broad-spectrum anti-inflammatory without damaging the immune system more, Sen-Jam is able to proactively change the course of inflammation for more than half the world. And inflammation comes in several forms: acute, chronic, autoimmune, and low grade chronic inflammation. We believe we can protect the immune system by preventing and reducing the initial cascade of inflammation that occurs, whether from our environment (diet, stress, allergies, substances of abuse, etc) or from disease (cardiometabolic, autoimmune or cancer).

What advice would you give

to aspiring pharmacists and entrepreneurs looking to make a difference in the pharmaceutical industry?

I believe that history repeats itself, and all the large pharmaceutical companies were initially started by a pharmacist, with an idea. And entrepreneurs are filled with new ideas infused with creativity. I believe that is where it begins, and then you start walking that path and learning how to do it your unique way. The industry is massive, and there are a lot of opportunities with some hard work. So your passion has to be your calling. Don't be afraid to bring a fresh mind to these large entrenched problems. In fact, we believe Einstein had it right when he said "you cannot solve a problem with the same consciousness that created it." Trust your instincts when something seems off to you and follow the data fiercely. The industry needs creative problem solvers like you so go out there and explore what's possible. Expect to face adversity, especially where money is holding the power in the room, but have conviction in your beliefs (and your data!) and always do your best.

Can you provide more details about Sen-Jam Pharmaceutical's recent partnership with a pharmaceutical manufacturer, Manufacturing & Controls (CMC), of your anti-inflammatory injectable, and how this collaboration will impact your product development and distribution?

Our partnership with KVK-Tech is a massive accelerant to our drug development activities. By working closely and early with our incredibly capable colleagues at this world-class manufacturing and controls organization, we are able to produce the highest quality product in the most efficient means possible. KVK and Sen-Jam forged an initial partnership around our oral mast cell modulator and recently entered a third drug development project together with the plans of developing the first mast cell modulating injectable for hospital use. We believe this product offers a much needed tool for physicians to transform care in that setting.

EMPOWERS ENTREPRENEURS

The Insights and Wisdom of CELIA SOONETS

Celia Soonets, market research expert turned author, discusses entrepreneurship, fear management, and her acclaimed book, 'The Wheel of 8 Fears of Entrepreneurs', offering practical strategies for success.

CELIA SOONETS

THE WHEEL OF 8 FEARS OF ENTREPRENEURS

A Practical Guide to Recognize and Overcome the Fear to Entrepreneurship

Discover 'The Wheel of 8 Fears of Entrepreneurs' by Celia Soonets—a transformative guide to mastering fears and maximizing business potential.

Entrepreneur Prime Magazine presents an in-depth exploration into the remarkable journey of Celia Soonets, a distinguished figure whose career spans over three decades across diverse domains of market research, entrepreneurship, and consultancy. Armed with degrees in Arts and Social Psychology from the Central University of Venezuela and an MBA from UQAM, Soonets initially honed her skills in corporate environments, rising through the ranks to hold pivotal roles in market research and marketing strategy. Her tenure in the corporate world provided invaluable insights into consumer behavior and business dynamics, laying a solid foundation for her subsequent entrepreneurial ventures.

In 2006, Celia Soonets diversified her professional portfolio by launching Soonets Jewelry, a micro-business that fused her artistic sensibilities with entrepreneurial acumen. This venture not only showcased her creativity but also underscored her ability to thrive independently in the competitive market landscape. Her entrepreneurial spirit further flourished with the inception of "Eslabones de Negocio," a Spanish-language blog tailored for micro-entrepreneurs, where she disseminates practical wisdom on values, attitudes, and habits conducive to entrepreneurial success.

However, it was in 2019 that Soonets embarked on a pivotal endeavor that would crystallize her expertise in entrepreneurship—publishing her seminal work, *The Wheel of 8 Fears of Entrepreneurs*. This groundbreaking book represents a culmination of her extensive research and practical experience, offering a structured framework to understand and confront the fears that often inhibit entrepreneurial progress. Drawing from her background in psychology and business, Soonets identifies eight core fears prevalent among entrepreneurs and provides actionable strategies to mitigate their impact.

Central to Soonets's approach is the recognition that fear, far from being a deterrent, serves as a critical signal for entrepreneurs navigating uncertain terrain. By reframing fear as a natural response to challenges and opportunities, she empowers her readers to harness this emotion constructively, transforming it into a catalyst for growth and innovation. Through a series of self-reflection exercises and practical tools embedded within the book, entrepreneurs are encouraged to confront their fears, dissect their origins, and devise personalized strategies to overcome them.

The impact of Soonets's work extends beyond theoretical insights, resonating deeply with entrepreneurs at various stages of their journey. Feedback from readers and professionals underscores the book's accessibility, practicality, and transformative potential. Many attest to its role in fostering resilience, enhancing decision-making, and nurturing a mindset conducive to sustained entrepreneurial success.

As a certified EMP Practitio-ner and a seasoned consultant, Soonets continues to advocate for a holistic approach to entrepreneurship—one that embraces vulnerability, adapts to change, and thrives amidst uncertainty. Her contributions not only enrich the entrepreneurial ecosystem but also inspire a new generation of business leaders to confront challenges with courage and creativity.

In conclusion, Celia Soonets exemplifies the blend of academic rigor, entrepreneurial spirit, and compassionate mentorship that defines contemporary entrepreneurship. Her journey from corporate executive to prolific author and consultant underscores her unwavering commitment to empowering entrepreneurs worldwide. Through her insights, Soonets continues to shape the narrative of entrepreneurial fear, positioning it not as a barrier, but as a transformative force essential for personal and professional growth in today's dynamic business landscape.

Dr. Obioma Martin's Inspirational Journey Toward Transformation

Dr. Obioma Martin partners with SuccessBooks® to co-author "Against All Odds", offering resilience-filled narratives. Her leadership and advocacy uplift ndividuals worldwide.

In the dynamic world of entrepreneurship and leadership, alliances are forged, and collaborations are celebrated. This Summer of 2024 brings forth a collaboration of extraordinary minds as Dr. Obioma Martin joins forces with SuccessBooks® to co-author the eagerly awaited book, "Against All Odds", alongside the esteemed Lisa Nichols and a remarkable ensemble of authors.

Scheduled to hit the shelves soon, "Against All Odds" is poised to captivate readers with narratives brimming with resilience, fortitude, and tenacity, promising to inspire and uplift audiences worldwide.

Dr. Obioma Martin stands as a luminary in the realms of Early Childhood Education, Entrepreneurship, and Leadership. Her impressive repertoire includes titles such as business strategist, Accountability Coach, keynote speaker, Transformational Facilitator, and Lisa Nichols Certified Transformational Trainer. With a fervent dedication to nurturing growth and facilitating transformative learning experiences, Dr. Martin has cemented her position as a seven-time Amazon best-selling author and a compelling TEDx Speaker, touching countless lives with her poignant narratives and actionable insights.

At the helm of OMAX Institute, Dr. Martin leads the charge in the Center for Early Childhood Education, Entrepreneurship, and Leadership, empowering individuals to unleash their full potential. Through her leadership at OmazingYou, she advocates for the power of personal storytelling, enabling individuals to inspire and uplift others. Moreover, Dr. Martin's commitment to societal betterment shines through her founding of OMART Women Supporting Women, a nonprofit organization dedicated to aiding battered women with children and teen parents.

Beyond her entrepreneurial ventures, Dr. Martin spearheads Obioma Martin LLC, leveraging her expertise in strategy and leadership to drive change and foster excellence. Her unwavering commitment to integrity, reliability, and dependability forms the cornerstone of her successful partnerships and professional endeavors.

Dr. Martin's academic credentials underscore her multifaceted approach to leadership and human relationships. With a doctorate in philosophy and certifications in trauma and biblical counseling, she embodies empathy and dedication to bringing healing and hope to those in need. As a John Maxwell certified leadership coach and speaker, she mentors emerging leaders, guiding them towards realizing their utmost potential.

In academia, Dr. Martin's scholarly prowess is reinforced by master's degrees in early childhood education and leadership, positioning her as an esteemed authority in her domain. Her ordination as an evangelist reflects her commitment to spiritual service and her ability to inspire and guide her community through faith and wisdom.

Dr. Obioma Martin epitomizes the essence of transformational leadership—a beacon of hope, a catalyst for change, and a steadfast support for those defying all odds.

To delve deeper into Dr. Martin's journey and her forthcoming collaboration in "Against All Odds", visit Obioma.org.

SuccessBooks® warmly welcomes Dr. Obioma Martin as a co-author of "Against All Odds". Stay tuned for the release of this transformative book, poised to embolden and empower readers through the collective stories of Dr. Obioma Martin, Lisa Nichols, and an exceptional team of author

Healing Beyond Boundaries

SAMANTHA JAYNE

Empowers Individuals To Reclaim Their Lives Through Transformative Spiritual Coaching And Healing

Samantha Jayne shares her journey as a multi-dimensional trance healer, highlighting transformative client success stories and her unique approach to spiritual coaching.

BY EDITOR'S DESK | LONDON

" We've established clear sustainability goals and ensure that all of our suppliers meet strict standards through audits and certifications."

Samantha Jayne stands as a beacon of hope and transformation in the realm of spiritual healing and coaching. With over 23 years of experience as a multi-dimensional trance healer, she has dedicated her life to guiding individuals on their journeys towards self-discovery and empowerment. Her unique ability to heal clients' energetic timelines and shift their mindsets has enabled countless business owners to step fully into their purpose, embracing the lives they were meant to lead. Samantha's resilience is particularly inspiring; after losing everything during the pandemic, she rebuilt her business from the ground up, achieving remarkable success in just three years. Her accolades, including recognition as one of the top 15 coaches in the world by CEO Weekly, underscore her profound impact on the landscape of success and personal growth.

Transitioning from her impressive journey, Samantha's insights into the transformative power of her work are both enlightening and inspiring. In our conversation, she shares specific success stories that highlight the profound changes her clients experience, as well as the personal journey that informs her coaching philosophy. Through her unique approach, she not only addresses the challenges her clients face but also empowers them to break free from ancestral patterns and embrace their true potential.

Can you share a specific success story where your coaching or healing methods significantly transformed someone's personal or professional life?

A client came to me because her children had been taken into care from her two years previously through false accusations and despite doing everything she was asked to do, she still was unable to get her children back home. She felt as if she was cursed and questioned if there was something 'dark' attached to her.

As I read for her on the situation spirit guided me to carry out my Karmic Cleanse Therapy ™.

Through this session we identified that this was in fact an ancestral karmic pattern and that this scenario was locked deep in the 'secrets' within the family.

I worked with this client to clear her of the ancestral karmic debts, the programming and the negative attachment that had formed because of this history.

I also cleared the home of the negative energy and entities holding such dark times in this space.

The transformation was almost instant and three months later I received a message telling me that they had agreed to send her children home to her. I felt so emotional to read those words. To know that I had played my part in healing the whole family and not just my clients. That these children were coming home to a Mum who loved them very much.

How has your personal journey of overcoming ancestral trauma and generational programming shaped your professional approach to coaching and healing?

Through my own journey of clearing the Ancestral programming around being a single mum and money I have been able to release myself from the relentless bust and boom cycle that I feel so many business owners experience. The majority of the work is done at a deep, inner level, as well as within the conscious and subconscious mindset. Through my own experiences, I am a guiding light for my coaching clients as I walk them through their own journey of letting go of the blocks to abundance. I show them how to take the path that will move them from blocked to blessed.

What inspired you to create VIBE, your coaching program for heart-centered entrepreneurs, and what unique elements does it offer compared to other coaching programs?

VIBE is the product of my work as a Spiritual Business Coach for the last 7 years. I know that so many light-workers, healers, therapists, teachers, readers, trainers, those who are here to be the difference in the world struggle with the programming about being spiritual and wealthy so I wanted to create a space where they can have access to affordable coaching.

I see too many genuine Healers and Therapist abandoning their gifts because they are blocked through 3D mind programming and because they have no business know-how.

In VIBE I show them how to manifest their dream business whilst fulfilling their purpose and creating their own rich life.

How do you stay updated

with the latest developments and trends in the spiritual and coaching industries?

Whilst I am a fully qualified Entrepreneur and Spiritual Coach, I don't follow trends. I see so many Coaches doing this to money-jack trends and for me this screams that coaching is not actually their purpose in this world. What I do, do though, is continue to develop myself spiritually and personally so that I can pass that knowledge on.

How has your approach to spiritual coaching evolved since you first started in the field?

My coaching has evolved to be far more energy, visionary and vibration based now than strategy based. It is also not about hitting six figures, it is about creating your own personal version of what a rich life looks like because that is abundance, that is love.

What role does intuition play in your business decisions, and how do you balance it with more traditional business strategies?

Intuition is everything! I teach this as part of my coaching.

What strategies do you employ to maintain boundaries while working with clients on deeply personal spiritual matters?

I maintain strong energetic boundaries. As a Heyoka Empath it is essential that I do. I also ensure I am scheduling self care time and encourage all my clients to do so too.

In what ways do you think the increased interest in spirituality since the pandemic has changed the industry?

The pandemic was the great awakening. A time of opportunity. Opportunity for us to unplug from generations of conditioning and open our minds to choosing to live in different ways. To want something different in life. The increase is spirituality is a hug indicator of this as people know they need to learn to go within for those answers. To find a new way of being and experiencing this world.

The Journey of an Inspiring Biotech Leader
RIKA TAJIMA
Pioneering Precision Medicine at Red Arrow Therapeutics

R ika Tajima stands at the intersection of cutting-edge nanotechnology and strategic leadership, guiding Red Arrow Therapeutics towards groundbreaking advancements in cancer treatment. Bilingual in English and Japanese, and an expert in corporate strategy and operations, Rika brings a wealth of experience from her diverse background in epidemiology, biostatistics, and global pharma environments. Her pivotal role in the successful M&A and post-merger integration projects showcases her strategic acumen and operational prowess.

Red Arrow Therapeutics, co-founded by Takuya Miyazaki and Horacio Cabral in 2021, aims to revolutionize cancer treatment through innovative drug delivery systems. Horacio's pioneering work on pH-sensitive nanopolymers, designed to deliver potent cancer drugs directly to tumor sites while sparing healthy cells, serves as the foundation of Red Arrow's mission. This vision of precision medicine inspired Takuya to translate this cutting-edge technology from the lab to patient care, forming the core mission of Red Arrow: delivering life-saving treatments with pinpoint accuracy.

Rika's journey from health economics research to co-founding Red Arrow reflects her passion for applying scientific rigor to real-world challenges. Her experience in health technology assessment and real-world data utilization in Japan provided a robust foundation for her transition into the fast-paced world of entrepreneurship. The dynamic environment of startups, characterized by rapid decision-ma-

king and resource optimization, captivated her during her tenure at Astellas Pharma, where she witnessed firsthand the impact of nimble, innovative approaches in the biotech sector.

Joining Red Arrow in 2023, Rika's multifaceted role encompasses fundraising, human resources, and clinical study design. Her leadership style emphasizes open communication, team collaboration, and maintaining a delicate balance between scientific innovation and business acumen. Rika fosters a culture of transparency and support, encouraging her team to voice their ideas and concerns, ensuring a cohesive and motivated workforce.

Rika's insights for aspiring entrepreneurs in the biotech and pharmaceutical sectors highlight the importance of recognizing one's strengths and seeking complementary partners. The intricate and highly regulated nature of these industries demands a collaborative approach, leveraging diverse expertise to navigate the complex journey from innovation to market.

In this exclusive interview with Entrepreneur Prime Magazine, Rika Tajima delves into the mission of Red Arrow Therapeutics, her transformative career path, and the leadership philosophies that drive her to shape the future of cancer treatment.

Rika Tajima discusses her journey from epidemiology to co-founding Red Arrow Therapeutics, emphasizing strategic leadership and innovative nanotechnology in cancer treatment.

What is the mission of Red Arrow Therapeutics? What inspired its founding?

Many known substances have high potential as drugs for cancer which currently cannot be treated, however they often harm healthy cells as side effects while targeting cancer cells. Horacio Cabral, a professor at the University of Tokyo and a world-leading researcher in nanomedicine, invented pH-sensitive nanopolymers that encapsulate such powerful drugs. These polymers form a protective shell around the drug, creating a molecule akin to an egg. When systemically injected, these molecules travel through the body to the target cancer site. The shell protects the healthy organs from the drug's effects. Once at the cancer site, where the pH is lower than the rest of the body, the shell breaks and releases the potent drug. The drug recruits immune cells to the cancer site, working together to destroy the cancer. These eggs act like a nano-sized Trojan horse within your body.

However, transforming cutting-edge technology into patient-ready treatments is a challenging journey. Takuya Miyazaki, who earned his PhD in Horacio's lab, recognized this and was inspired to bridge this gap.

He decided to start a company to nurture Horacio's groundbreaking technology as swiftly and efficiently as possible, leveraging resources from around the world. And hence, Red Arrow Therapeutics was co-founded by Takuya and Horacio in 2021, with the mission to save lives by delivering drugs bulls-eye.

Can you share your journey from your early career in health economics research to co-founding Red Arrow Therapeutics? What motivated you to transition into entrepreneurship?

My background is in epidemiology and biostatistics. Applying scientific and strategic thinking to real-world practice and making a tangible difference has always been a driving force for me. I thrive on daily collaborations with dynamic people to tackle new challenges. This led me to explore uncharted territories, such as the initial adoption of Health Technology Assessment in Japan and the use of real-world data in Japanese regulator-required post-marketing safety studies. Through these experiences, I learned to manage stakeholder expectations, influence without authority, and keep teams motivated amid uncertainty.

I was introduced to entrepreneurship while part of the

R&D collaboration team between Astellas Pharma and iota Biosciences, a MedTech startup in California. This collaboration eventually led to Astellas acquiring iota. Witnessing the speed and flexibility of the startup environment compared to big pharma was eye-opening. The process of prioritizing limited resources to find optimal solutions through speedy trial and error was exhilarating.

Around this time, I met Takuya and Horacio. Takuya's quick thinking and enthusiasm, and Horacio's sincerity and ardentness towards his research intrigued me. I admired the technology and felt that my problem-solving skills and a wide spectrum of experience in pharma would be a great addition to the team. Moreover, I wanted to challenge myself in a smaller organization to see if I could make a more significant impact. I now realize that, in a startup, you can, or inevitably end up doing everything, which feels more hands-on. I joined Red Arrow in 2023, contributing as a jack-of-all-trades in areas from fundraising, human resources, to clinical study design, and eventually became a co-founder.

As a co-founder and VP, what have been some of the most significant challenges you've faced in building and growing Red Arrow Therapeutics, and how have you overcome them? How would you describe your leadership style, and how do you foster a positive and productive culture within your team?

I've heard a saying that more than half of biotech failures are a result of operational challenges rather than scientific/technical challenges. One of the most significant challenges has been building and maintaining a strong team. The size and expertise level of the team must be necessary and sufficient at different points in time to remain nimble and financially prudent. The impact of each team member is vast compared to larger organizations. Additionally, startups are high-stress environments: volatile and demanding.

Above all, I try to be a good communicator, especially a good listener. Many leaders are adept at expressing their opinions, but not everyone feels comfortable speaking up towards them. What needs to be said in the best interest of the company may not be the most comfortable. I strive to create an environment where team members feel safe to straight-talk. I also value being open about what I don't know and asking for help in a speedy manner. Having a diverse network of mentors has been invaluable through by startup journey. Additionally, timely communication is crucial.

As a leader, I value maintaining a balanced focus on both the science and the business. Ultimately, a sense of contributing to patients and making the world a better place get me up in the morning, and I aim to share this sense of purpose with the team, fostering pride in our work.

What advice would you give to aspiring entrepreneurs, especially those looking to enter the biotech and pharmaceutical sectors?

Biotech and pharma are unique within the startup space. They are patent-driven, highly regulated, and require years to generate revenue, unlike consumer products. This niche demands a myriad of expertise. No one person can cover every necessary skill. Identify your strengths and weaknesses, find complementary partners, and let's get started!

Rika Tajima, co-founder and VP of Red Arrow Therapeutics, leading the charge in innovative cancer treatments through nanotechnology.

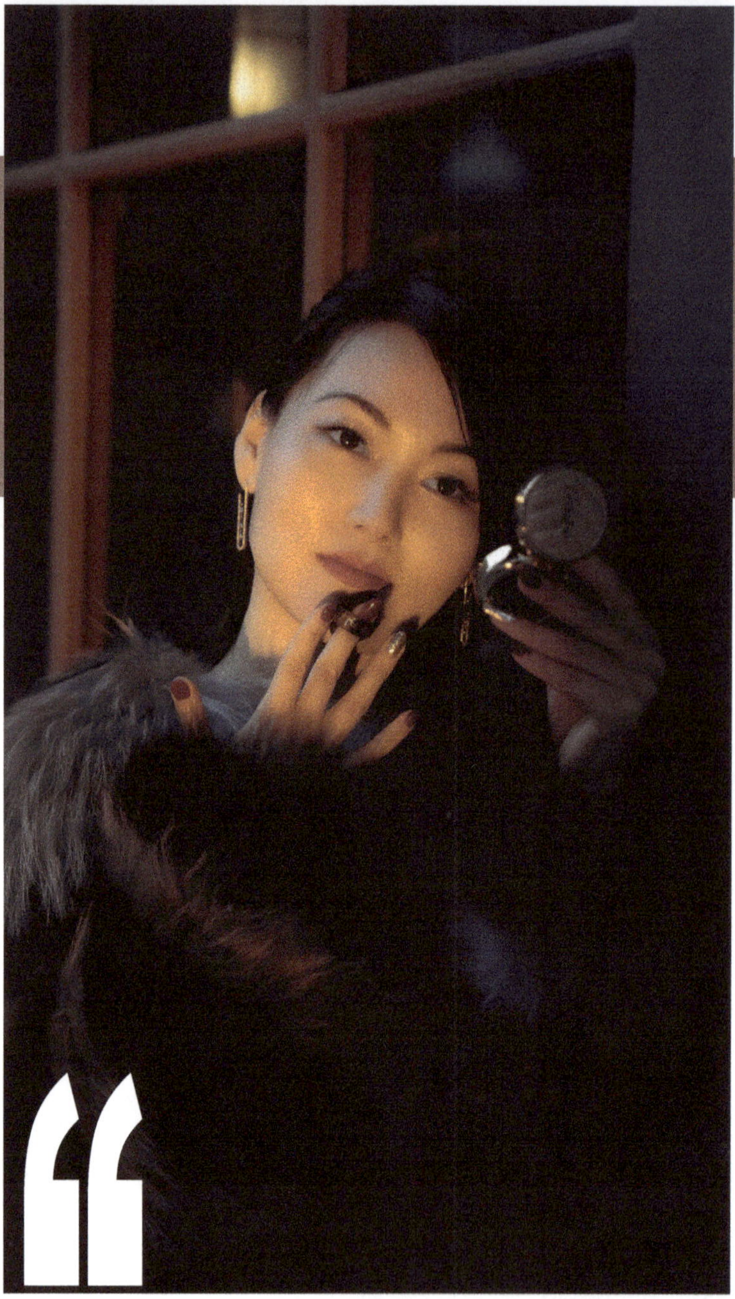

Yuhan Liu discusses her transition from journalism to entrepreneurship, her role in promoting Chinese designers globally, and her commitment to sustainability and cultural integration in fashion.

YUHAN LIU

DISCOVER HOW YUHAN IS ELEVATING CHINESE DESIGNERS ON THE INTERNATIONAL STAGE

as told to H. HITOMI

"

Yuhan Liu, co-founder of the China Fashion Collective, champions Chinese designers on the global stage with her innovative vision and leadership.

Yuhan Liu is a visionary force in the fashion industry, seamlessly blending her journalistic prowess with entrepreneurial acumen to elevate Chinese designers on the global stage. As the co-founder of the China Fashion Collective, Liu has been instrumental in providing a platform for emerging talents to showcase their creativity at prestigious events like New York Fashion Week. Her journey from a successful journalism career to becoming a celebrated entrepreneur is a testament to her dedication and passion for bridging cultural divides through fashion. Recognized as one of the Forbes China 100 Most Influential Overseas Chinese, Liu's work continues to inspire and pave the way for future generations of designers.

In this exclusive interview with Entrepreneur Prime Magazine, Yuhan Liu shares her motivations for transitioning from journalism to entrepreneurship and how her experiences have shaped her leadership of the China Fashion Collective. She discusses the impact of her recognition by Forbes, the challenges and opportunities faced by her organization, and her commitment to promoting sustainability within the fashion industry. Liu also offers insights into her long-term goals for the China Fashion Collective and her vision for its evolving role in the global fashion scene. Join us as we delve into the mind of a trailblazer who is redefining the boundaries of fashion and culture.

What motivated you to transition from a successful journalism career to entrepreneurship, and how have your experiences in journalism influ-

"Fashion is not just about clothing; it's a powerful medium for storytelling and cultural exchange."
— Yuhan Liu

Yuhan Liu is a trailblazer, elevating Chinese fashion globally with her visionary leadership and commitment to cultural integration.

...enced your approach to leading the China Fashion Collective?

Soon after beginning my career at the New York branch of China Daily in 2011, I had the opportunity to cover a New York Fashion Show in the heart of Manhattan. It was a group fashion show featuring designers from Shenzhen, China's fashion industry hub. I was amazed by the immense talent of Chinese designers and felt that they truly deserved a global platform like New York Fashion Week to showcase their creativity.

Following my time at China Daily, I joined a Mandarin-English bilingual fashion and lifestyle magazine under Observer Media in midtown Manhattan, New York, where I served as Managing Editor. This role gave me even deeper insights into the fashion and media industries. With my bilingual and bicultural background, combined with my professional experience, I realized that I could help emerging designers, brands, and industry professionals gain international visibility.

In 2017, I joined hands with my former colleague from the Observer Claire Lin and established China Fashion Collective. We produced a show for Cai Meiyue, China's top bridal designer, at Pier 59. From that point, China Fashion Collective truly took off.

In conclusion, I'm incredibly grateful for my journalism career at China Daily, Observer Media, and The New York Times, and I love my current role as an entrepreneur as well. These two aspects of my life—journalism and entrepreneurship—bring me immense joy and fulfillment every day.

Being recognized as one of the Forbes China 100 Most Influential Overseas Chinese is a significant achievement. How has this recognition impacted your work and your vision for the future of the China Fashion Collective and your other ventures?

This award is a prestigious recognition and I feel lucky to be included. Honestly, the recognition does boost the credibility in both Chinese and international markets on personal level and on the business level.

It helps me build trust with friends, industry counterparts and clients more easily, so I'm very grateful for the recognition. This also opened doors for valuable partnerships, collaborations,

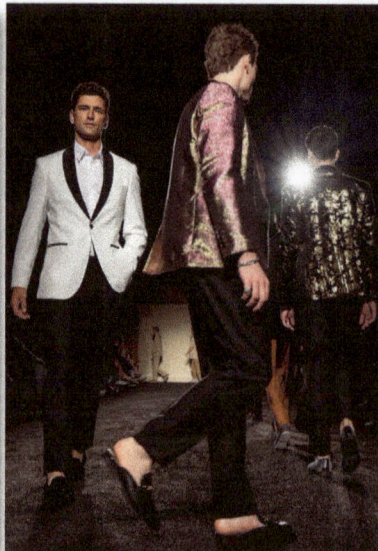

"My background in journalism taught me to look beyond the surface, to seek the stories that garments can tell."
– Yuhan Liu

PHOTO: *Yuhan Liu, drawing from her rich journalism background, brings a unique storytelling perspective to the fashion industry, bridging cultures and narratives through her work.*
Photos courtesy of China Fashion Collective

and new opportunities for expansion in both China and the US. Although the recognition only comes after 11 years of hard work, I found it inspiring and motivating to continue the hard work. Being a better self, a better entrepreneur.

What inspired the creation of The China Fashion Collective, and what is the primary mission you aim to achieve with this initiative?

I was amazed by the immense talent of Chinese designers and felt that they need a global platform like New York Fashion Week to showcase their creativity. And New York is the perfect place to bring people and culture together, it's

one of the most embracing cities in the world. China Fashion Collective just recently did a New York Fashion Week show at the iconic Cipriani in downtown Manhattan, we showcased 60 pieces for Amazon's top menswear seller

Coofandy and women's sleepwear Ekouaer which turned out to be a big success.

Our mission is to deliver exceptional quality and design to a global audience, making it accessible for everyone to experience. In today's connected world, boundaries no longer limit creativity.

In what ways does The China Fashion Collective aim to showcase and integrate Chinese culture and heritage into the global fashion scene?

• Enpowering emerging Chinese designers on the global platform;

• Encouraging up-and-coming designers collaborate with international talents and designers for more sparks in the art of fashion;

• Promoting green-fashion/sustainable fashion concepts to our community.

What are some of the biggest challenges you have faced in establishing The China Fashion Collective, and what opportunities do you see for its growth in the future?

The biggest challenges we faced were during the pandemic from 2020 to 2022, when the whole world, including China Fashion Collective, came to a standstill. However, as the world recovers, China's talents, artists, businesses, designers..are once again pursuing international visibility and expanding into global markets. This resurgence presents an ideal opportunity for China Fashion Collective as well.

Following the success of our September show, we've already received inquiries for the February show and branding opportunities for Q4. With so much on our plate, New York continues to offer tremendous opportunities for international businesses like ours.

How does The China Fashion Collective address sustainability within the fashion industry, and what steps are being taken to promote eco-friendly practices among participating designers?

Good question. One of our clients, Kokolu, is a brand I'm especially proud to work with. They produce fashion items such as sneakers, hats, and tote bags, and more; I'm a huge fan of their products—I still use their sneakers and nylon-like tote bags made entirely from recycled post-consumer plastic bottles. Kokolu is committed to using only environmentally friendly materials, and sustainability is truly at the core of their brand. We, on behalf of Kokolu, worked with

Alexix Ren, one of the most influential personalities on social media (under EWG Management)

to promote the idea of using sustainable-material-made fashion items among her 18 million followers.

Recently I've been invited by Amazon Shanghai, Amazon Shenzhen, SohoWork and other platforms for panels, and I always take the opportunity to highlight Kokolu's story and their dedication to sustainability. As the fashion industry is one of the largest contributors to global warming, I believe China Fashion Collective also has a responsibility to promote sustainable values to our audience and partners.

What are your long-term goals for The China Fashion Collective, and how do you envision its role evolving in the global fashion industry over the next few years?

• Promote sustainability values to designers and brands;

• Help emerging designers from Asia continue to gain international visibility;

• Foster more international collaborations;

How do you incorporate elements of Chinese culture and heritage into your designs, and what aspects are most important to you?

Actually many of our designers are Parsons Grads, or Central Saint Martins Grads, or top design schools from Asia, many of them are young and international citizens, only a very small number of them infuse some Chinese elements into the design, so that's probably not our focus :)

Leading with Vision and
Empowering Aesthetics

ALYSSA RAPP

EMPOWERS WOMEN ENTREPRENEURS IN THE MEDICAL AESTHETICS INDUSTRY

Alyssa Rapp, CEO of Empower Aesthetics and bestselling author, shares her journey of leadership and empowerment in the medical aesthetics industry.

As of January 2018, Alyssa was named the CEO of Empower Aesthetics by private equity firm Sterling Partners. Within six months, she was named one of Crain's Chicago's "Notable Women in Health Care" (June 2018). Starting in 2014, Alyssa joined the ranks as a lecturer-in-management at Stanford University's Graduate School of Business. As of June 2019, she was also named an Adjunct Professor of Entrepreneurship at the University of Chicago's Booth Business School.

From 2005-2015, Alyssa served as the founder & CEO of Bottlenotes, Inc., the leading interactive media company in the U.S. wine, craft beer, and artisanal spirit industries.

Starting in 2015, Alyssa has also served as the Managing Partner at AJR Ventures, a strategic advisory firm for Fortune 500, $500MM+ privately-held companies, and private equity firms on their new business unit/new market development, digital and e-commerce strategies.

Alyssa was named in Inc. Magazine's "30 Under 30" coolest entrepreneurs in America (September 2008)" and one of the wine industry's top 25 of 100 most influential people by Intowine.com, from 2012 to present. Bottlenotes also received the "Best Advertising and Marketing Company" and the "People's Choice Award" at the Empact 100 in September 2013 at the United Nations, honoring the top 100 companies with founders under 35.

Alyssa earned a B.A. in Political Science and the History of Art from Yale University in 2000 and an M.B.A. from Stanford University's Graduate School of Business in 2005. At Yale, she earned the Frank M. Patterson prize for the best essay on the American political system for her senior thesis on public housing reform in Chicago. Alyssa is thus honored to have been appointed by Illinois Governor Bruce Rauner to serve on the board of directors of the Illinois Housing Development Authority. She currently serves on the organization's audit committee with $1B of assets and ~$80MM operating expenses.

When not immersed in business and civic life, Alyssa loves to run track,

do yoga, ski fast, and try as hard as possible to decipher a slider from a curve ball from her husband, 1990 MLB World Series champion and partner at X10 Capital, Hal Morris. Alyssa and Hal are the proud parents of Audrey Margaret Morris and Henriette Daniella Morris.

Empower Aesthetics aims to inspire joy and confidence through aesthetics. Can you

Alyssa Rapp exemplifies visionary leadership and entrepreneurial spirit, inspiring women to achieve excellence in business and beyond.

elaborate on what this means to you and how you implement this philosophy within the company?

There are two meanings implied by this tagline of sorts. For one, we hope and believe that preserving and enhancing one's physical beauty can provide our clients with more joy and at times, even more self-confidence. This is part one of the meaning of this tagline.

In addition, we are partnering with primarily women-entrepreneurs when we acquire their clinics as part of the Empower Aesthetics platform. In so doing, it is both fun and gratifying to shepherd these women stakeholders through the mergers and acquisitions process, inspiring them to join a platform that espouses their shared vision for the category, which of course we hope brings them joy and confidence via the partnership.

As a successful entrepreneur and CEO, what are the key challenges you face in the medical aesthetics industry, and how do you overcome them?

One of the key attractions to me of the CEO role at Empower is the opportunity to acquire companies founded and led by women entrepreneurs. Our target seller is a 45 – 65-year-old woman, who deeply values clinical excellence, the training of excellence in her team, and delivery of it to her clinic's patients. It is a key opportunity and challenge to successfully

convince these terrific women entrepreneurs that now is the right time to sell (partner) versus to continue to "go it alone," and why "us" versus a handful of other private-equity backed Medical Aesthetics platforms in the ecosystem. We have meaningfully differentiated reasons "why now" and "why us," but great entrepreneurs and clinical leaders don't "have" to do something today per se, so inspiring them to act and act now is a challenge we look forward to continuing to addressing.

Your book, "Leadership and Life Hacks," became an Amazon bestseller for leadership. What are some key insights from the book that you apply in your role at Empower Aesthetics?

There are several leadership "hacks" from the book that are relevant to me as the CEO of Empower Aesthetics, as it would be in most CEO roles (if not all). In my chapter on managing boards and other key stakeholders, I share some truisms such as "breaking bread matters" and "all relationships are bespoke." These insights and strategies for managing members of my executive team and members of my board of directors rings in each of my CEO roles to date. I am also continually reminded of the importance of mentorship and sponsorship as an organizational leader, which I discuss at length in the chapter of the book entitled "Be One, Get One: The Power of Mentorships." Additionally, I learned from one of my most important career mentors and sponsors, Joel Peterson, that values-based leadership is the kind to which the most talented people and best teammates are attracted; I continue to strive to follow in Joel's best in class example with this type of entrepreneurial leadership (to quote his book of the same name). In sum, alignment of mission, vision, and values is instrumental to any team's success, and this approach remains crucial to our approach at Empower Aesthetics.

What role have your family's values played in your professional journey?

My inspiration and the reason I serve on wonderful nonprofit or civic boards is due to the role modeling and values instilled by my mother and stepfather. They raised me and us to live a life of service. They both serve as role models to me in their lives of service (my mother having served as the former US Ambassador to the Netherlands, my stepfather as a real estate developer in Chicago for over a half-century, whose work, amongst many other things, not only shaped the city

PHOTO: The dynamic team at Empower Aesthetics, led by CEO Alyssa Rapp, driving innovation and excellence in the medical aesthetics industry.

of Chicago, but brought best in class management to its public housing). Through their actions and examples, they role model that "giving back" is simply what we do, with time and with treasure. And this has influenced several of the choices I have made throughout my professional journey on which nonprofit or civic boards I serve. Since I have always deeply valued the early childhood education and public education that I received growing up, I currently serve as an elected member the District 36 school board, for example.

What advice would you give to women aspiring to become CEOs, entrepreneurs, or leaders in their fields?

As Geena Davis said, "If you can see it, you can be it." As women are exposed to more and more great examples of women a CEOs, and leading entrepreneurs and executives, I am hopeful that the success of more and more women will continue to inspire women to keep striving, keep climbing, and keep leading at the highest of levels, in corporate America and on corporate boards. As for advice, there's several "hacks" previously discussed that are directly relevant to your question:

• Find inspirational mentors to learn from

• Support flexible work environments.

• If you're already in a leadership position, install qualified women in your organization and "Demand" (Strongly Recommend/Request) gender equity in the executive leadership teams and on the boards you serve E.g.: Walk the walk.

McKinsey's Women in the Workplace study spotlighted how women fall behind early in their careers, and that they are at a disadvantage in their daily interactions because they see fewer women around them. So, we need to support women getting promoted earlier in their careers and provide structures and environments that overtly support mentorship. For any person in a leadership role, but especially for a woman in a male-dominated industry, a strong professional network of women can help buoy you through proverbial storms.

The Influence of Heritage in Contemporary Art

> "Drawing is the basis of everything I do. It is like a hidden language that operates directly out of the nervous system."

DAVID OSBALDESTON

David explores the dynamic interplay of images and words through his innovative collage and printmaking techniques

David Osbaldeston discusses his artistic process, the significance of scale in his work, and the themes of identity and value in his upcoming publication.

David Osbaldeston, whose innovative approach to collage and printmaking invites viewers to reconsider the boundaries between words and images. Osbaldeston's work stands as a testament to the power of visual storytelling, marrying the spontaneity of collage with the meticulous craftsmanship of intaglio etching. Through his dynamic use of scale and material, he challenges traditional notions of value, class, and identity, creating a dialogue that resonates deeply with contemporary audiences.

Osbaldeston's artistic practice embodies a unique synthesis of historical influences and modern techniques, as he navigates the intricate relationships between disparate elements. His belief that drawing is a hidden language that operates from within the nervous system permeates his work, revealing the layered complexities of identity and perception. With a keen eye for the interplay of forms, he transforms the act of making into a form of social commentary, inviting us to reflect on our own positions within the fabric of society. In this exclusive interview, Osbaldeston shares insights into his creative process, the significance of scale, and the motivations behind his upcoming publication, "A Pastiche of Different Techniques." Prepare to be inspired by an artist whose work is as thought-provoking as it is visually stunning.

How does collage serve as a medium for exploring the relationships between images and words in your work?

It's a way to put images together. Words are images. My interest in collage deals simply with the re-arrangement of separate realities.

It is a form of open play, so I think with my hands as much as my head. I'm always prepared

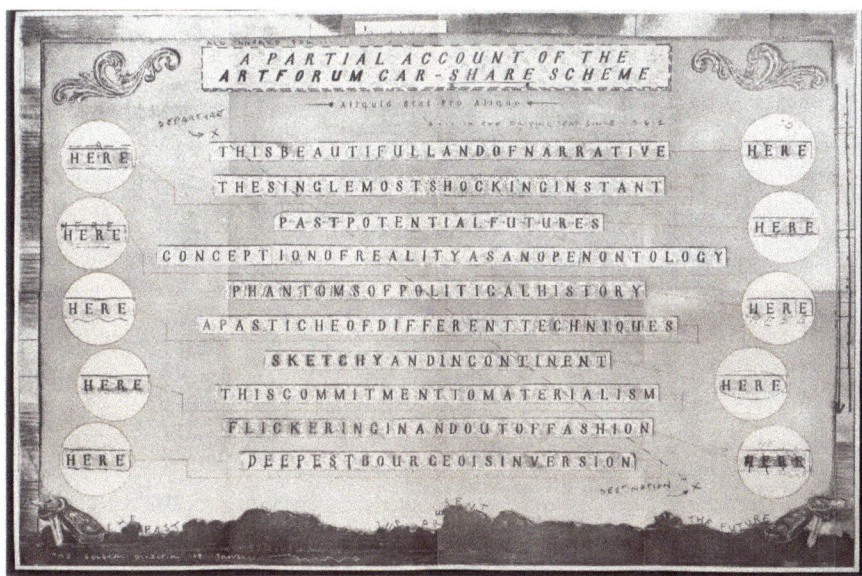

A stunning display of David Osbaldeston's large-scale intaglio etchings and collaged paintings, highlighting the intricate relationships between images and words.

David Osbaldeston's innovative approach and mastery of collage reveal profound insights into identity and perception, captivating audiences with every piece.

for the collages to not work out, but the ones that do often end up as large-scale intaglio etchings. I don't enjoy making things difficult, but the paradox between the spontaneity of collage and the slowness of etching creates a tension that becomes an essential part of the message. The priority is in making the right word and image work together. It's the same with the 'word prop' series I have been making on prepared linen which are screen prints.

Can you discuss the significance of scale in your artwork, particularly regarding your artist's books versus your large-scale etchings?

I discovered a long time ago that I like to work at opposite ends of scale. Sometimes an idea will be best suited to the modest scale of an artist's book where it makes more sense for the work and the reader to be in sync.

Other times when I embark on a large etching, I find myself obsessing over how an image occupies space almost like a piece of sculpture. For my first solo show I made a composite etching to fit the surface area of a billboard where the intimacy of it on such a scale invited a closer form of visual reading.

What role does drawing play in your artistic process, and how does it inform the other media you engage with?

Drawing is the basis of everything I do. It is like a hidden language that operates directly out of the nervous system as an interaction. Each time I begin something, a different challenge always presents itself, but it always comes through drawing. I consider drawing as something other than simply making pictorial observations.

You mention a desire to challenge perceptions of value, class, and identity. How do these themes manifest in your work?

Fine art practice is generally rooted in perceptions and realities of remoteness and exclusivity. I like to work with opposites of process. Etching is thought of as a substitute for painting. Screen

printing evolved from an industrial process, and so on... The irony is I don't see myself as a printmaker, but much of my interest stems from a desire to satirise the assumptions of what an art object might be which is probably a very bourgeoise idea in itself.

I'm not attempting to identify as a working-class artist, but I understand it. Like many others, my mother came to post-war England from rural Ireland with no qualifications and held it together for most her working life as a carer and hospital cleaner. After lots of jobs my dad worked for a while as a librarian in F.E but due to mental health issues decided to opt out in his forties. We had no money. Growing up I was acutely aware of how that feels, and it never leaves you.

What motivated you to create the upcoming book "A Pastiche of Different Techniques," and what can audiences expect from it?

The book charts the development of studio work I've made over the last two years for solo exhibitions at Glasgow Print Studio and Moon Grove in Manchester. I'm drawn to the idea of it extending their life and it will be an artist's book in the sense that it has a two-colour screen-printed dustjacket. The book will be published in early 2025 and tell the story of the work's development with images of recent etchings, screen prints on linen, and collaged paintings each made in series.

As you describe it. In what ways do you aim to create a porous relationship between your studio practice and the outside world through your exhibitions and publications?

I've come to think of what I make as 'flat sculpture' which is a way to describe how images and words are pushed together to make a compressed form. An artwork that slots through a letter box is still a very seductive idea, just as it can be when a work is made to be sited on a wall. But it's always material.

Dreams and Found Materials

Discovering the imaginative process behind Lee's unique, tactile creations

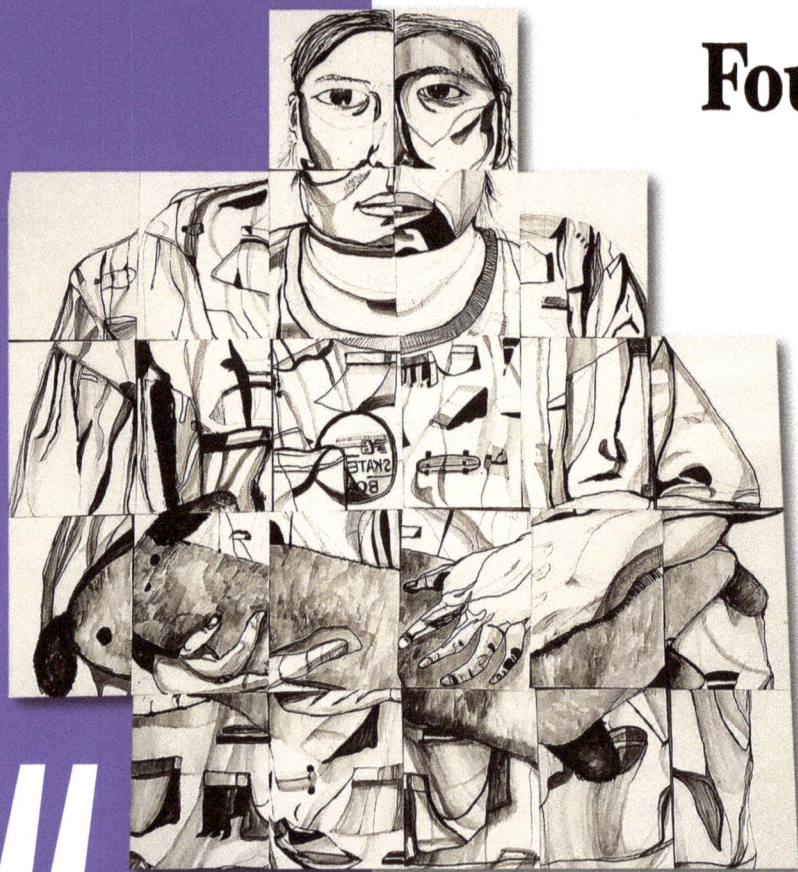

> "Drawing, painting and sculpting makes me remember what I enjoyed, when I felt a strong emotion, which lets me slow down in my present life."

JUNGMIN LEE

Jungmin Lee's art, inspired by childhood, dreams, and cultural heritage, blends personal and collective memory through mixed media, creating intimate, miniature worlds that celebrate family, tradition, and the timeless warmth of nostalgia.

Jungmin Lee's art transports us to a world rich with nostalgia, dreams, and the tactile warmth of memory. This talented South Korean artist and designer, a graduate with distinction from the ArtCenter College of Design, blends storytelling with a love for found and mixed media to create intricate, evocative pieces. Her works invite viewers into intimate moments of family gatherings, childhood explorations, and even dreamscapes—transforming everyday materials into portals to the past. Lee's creativity is steeped in the heritage of her culture, tracing her roots through memories of her grandparents' home, traditional rituals, and cherished heirlooms, reimagined into vivid visual narratives.

Throughout her work, Lee demonstrates a profound ability to weave together personal and collective memory. Her piece Cabinet, a layered collage of stamps, stickers, and pages from her mother's notebooks, powerfully bridges her own life and history with a broader cultural experience. With each brushstroke and piece of found material, she crafts a miniature world where fragments of her heritage live on. It is through these meticulously crafted "miniatures" that Lee explores themes of belonging, identity, and emotional resilience. In this exclusive interview, WOWwArt Magazine delves into the inspirations, creative process, and unique perspectives that make Jungmin Lee's art both intensely personal and universally resonant.

Can you describe how your childhood experiences in South Korea influence your artistic themes and subjects?

Jungmin Lee, an accomplished artist from Incheon, South Korea, finds inspiration in the whimsical realms of childhood, dreams, and family. A graduate with distinction from ArtCenter College of Design, her work beautifully blends found and mixed media, storytelling from cherished memories, and the tactile creation of 3D objects. Her art is a vivid tapestry of imagination and heartfelt narratives.

Jungmin Lee captivates audiences with her profound storytelling, transforming ordinary objects into extraordinary visual narratives that resonate with universal human warmth.

When I was young, my family liked to go on trips to visit big, old trees, such as the 800 year old Ginkgo tree in Jangsudong, Incheon, South Korea. In the beginning, I didn't know why we were going to see trees. But as time went by, these trips became my memory points to spiritually go back as the place of family gathering. This nostalgic warmth is also connected to my grandparents and visiting their home. I appreciate their time to cook delicious foods like Ramyun, soybean paste soup, seasoned spinach, and more. I remember when my grandparents brought small dogs to home on a cold winter evening. I remember when my family prepared food and visited the parents of my grandparents at the cemetery, covered with snow. These moments are living inside of me, and art helps to bring me the forgotten past. Because I am now far away from my grandparents, this childhood feels like a dream. Drawing, painting and sculpting makes me remember what I enjoyed, when I felt a strong emotion, which lets me slow down in my present life, and rethink why I want to study art.

What role do dreams play in your creative process, and how do you incorporate them into your work?

Dreams to me are uncertain, blurry, weird so it gives me open possibilities to experiment. It can be changed during the thinking process, or sometimes the new pieces of another dream come up after sleep. Memory is changing and they are fantastical. Anything can happen so I appreciate that dream gives me free ground to start from. It represents to me less pressure and motivates me to switch the storyline, draw without a plan, combine found materials, or maybe erase and restart.

How do you use mixed media in your artwork, and what materials do you find most inspiring?

I like to travel in my house to collect, find new materials, such as trash, recycle bins or old boxes in the garage. One day, I start with one object, then maybe the next day, I cut it out. Another day, I might paint over, or look over the magazine to find the image. I think I make it in the process with less plan, and I like to practice these experiments with different types and scales of the media. These days, I am also interested in learning more about watercolor and brush. I enjoy playing with water and unexpectedness with where the inks would go and share its feelings.

Can you explain your concept of a "miniature world" in your paintings and how it reflects collective and individual dynamics?

I think the practice of thinking about a "miniature" helps me to observe the world in a simple way or to view from a far away. The making process is also like playing with a toy or going back to when I was young. Inside of the miniature world, the creatures and houses seemed to feel safe and open a way to start an adventure. Miniature drawings or objects become able to hold in hands, move around, or invite me to make my own world. I think this process of creating a small environment gives a coziness and warmth to my mind, and I hope this feeling could help to share the playful spirits and healing aspects of art.

How do cultural backgrounds and customs shape the characters and narratives in your art?

From my memories in Korea, the traditional foods and ancestral rites with my family come to my mind. Often, my family members and their personality became my starting point to sketch the unknown creatures or my imaginary friend characters. In another moment, grandparents become the main characters who show me the steps of Jesa, Korean ancestral rituals, or as the biographed figure by interviewing with them. The folk tales and traditional music in Korea help me to learn where I come from, teach me new languages that were used in the past, or how ancestors lived their lives.

What psychological observations do you hope to convey through the interactions between collective power and individual power in your work?

To me, collective power guides me the sympathy that can be made with wider people, and individual power as the departure from the personal memory. My work can begin with my personal backgrounds or interactions within myself. But my bigger hope is to observe the influences of childhood to adulthood and the conflicted minds of people, which I like to try sharing this diverse human emotions in art so that one can feel connected or belong. I hope my work can help more people to dream and imagine, especially to feel free in their state of mind.

Redefining the American Dream

"

Every drawing of mine comes through transitional space. Otherwise it would be manufactured."

LINDA KARSHAN

Exploring How Linda Karshan Merges Psychological Theories With Artistic Expression To Create Works Of Profound Depth

Linda Karshan discusses the influence of psychology on her art, her rhythmic approach to creation, and how her unique methods invite viewers to engage with the essence of creativity.

We delve into the profound artistic journey of a true innovator whose works transcend traditional boundaries. Linda Karshan, an artist of exceptional depth and insight, merges the realms of psychology and art in a manner that resonates with both intellect and emotion. With a foundation built on her education at esteemed institutions such as the Sorbonne and the Slade School of Art, Karshan has cultivated a unique approach that reflects her extensive studies and experiences.

Her oeuvre, characterized by intricate drawings, prints, and artists' books, embodies a delicate balance between structure and organic expression. Karshan's exploration of transitional space and creative play, influenced by the psychological theories of D.W.

Winnicott, reveals an artist deeply engaged in the process of self-discovery and artistic expression. Her works invite viewers into a dialogue about the nature of creativity itself, challenging us to reconsider the boundaries of artistic practice. With exhibitions in prestigious museums and collections around the globe, including the British Museum and the Metropolitan Museum of Art, Karshan continues to inspire and captivate audiences with her evocative, rhythmically structured creations. This conversation offers a rare glimpse into her artistic philosophy and the dynamic interplay between movement, thought, and expression that defines her work.

How did your studies in psychology and Plato's theory of numerical order influence your performance-based artistic method?

Linda Karshan's mesmerizing creation embodies a perfect harmony of rhythm, structure, and organic expression. Each line, born from her 'inner choreography,' invites the viewer into a meditative dialogue on movement, time, and the essence of creativity.

In my work it's never a case of influence but of affinity.

My studies in psychology focused on Donald Winnicott, whose theories of transitional space and transitional phenomena are key to my artistic practice. Winnicott's theories gave me ballast, even courage, to stay in pace and place throughout the making of an artwork.

He wrote about creative play. It's a precarious place that hovers between the unconscious and consciousness. He said it was here and only here that anything original gets made, and so it is. Every drawing of mine comes through transitional space. Otherwise

Linda Karshan is a visionary artist whose profound exploration of transitional space and creative play resonates deeply, inspiring viewers and fellow creators alike.

it would be manufactured.

Plato found me.

I had made a suite of prints which became an artist's book, Time, Being; le temps, lui.

I asked my friend, the philosopher David Wiggins, to write an accompanying text. After inspecting the prints for thirty minutes, he said 'Ah, there is no need. The text exists. He sent me the passage from Plato's Timeus, on the creation of time.

As Mara Gerety wrote, 'she moves her body through each space.. marking out Plato's perfect numerical ordering of the universe.'

Can you describe the role that your concept "inner choreography" plays in the creation of your prints and drawings?

It is key. That inner choreography IS the moving figure assigned to me. It determines every drawing, on paper or in space. I can

count on it, literally and figuratively, and I do. It sounds like this:

1-2-3-4-5-6-7-8 turn

1-2-3-4-5-6-7-8 turn

It's what my body does, guided by my mind. It first appeared in the drawing I call my Self-Portrait. Crucially, the day it appeared I saw Quad, the teleplay by Samuel Beckett. It was as if I were watching my drawing performed on stage. Beckett remains the artist with whom I feel the closest affinity.

In 1994, you transitioned to a more structured, rhythmic approach in your art-making. What prompted this shift from expressive compositions to performance-based, iterative works?

The appearance of the moving figure, with its numbers, rhythm and direction to turn the sheet. When it came into being, I recognized it for what it was. Thanks to Winnicott I knew not to get in the way; not to impinge. Once this small, iconic drawing was done, I pinned it to the wall, caught my breath, and knew I could begin.

So it wasn't a transition I planned, but one that appeared. I immediately saw its significance. Yes, it is more structured, and it is rhythmic, but it is in the same breath organic.

How do the physical movements, such as turning the paper counter-clockwise and counting increments of time, contribute to the geometric patterns and grids in your work?

Two important things to say here. Perhaps my most original jotting goes like this: man marks himself vertically, it is the Earth that turns. That's how we make the grid, that's why we make the grid.

And so I have to turn the sheet. It's directive. I have no choice.

I do not make the line that you read as horizontal. It's another vertical line. And I never confuse my horizontals and my verticals.

So turning the sheet is absolutely key, and while I never thought that I make grids, of

course that's what they are. Horizontal and vertical lines, but they come into being as a result of the turn.

Your MA thesis explored D. W. Winnicott's theories of transitional space and creativity. How do these psychological concepts continue to shape your artistic practice today?

My thesis was called Play, Creativity, and the Birth of the Self. I believe in those things now more than ever. These ideas are at the heart of every drawing I make. They started with Winnicott, but developed through my artistic practice.

It's worth reiterating that Winnicott's ideas on transitional space are key to the artistic side of my work.

The other key is my Bauhaus training, in which I was taught to build a drawing, to cross those corners. The drawing should not fall apart when I get up close.

But Winnicott's insistence on creative space - it is here and only here that anything original gets made - is essential.

You've exhibited in major galleries and museums across Europe and the U.S. How do you feel your work has been received in these different cultural contexts?

That's a great question. There is a predisposition in certain cultural milieu, where my work can be seen and felt, because it's close to the experience of the viewer. It's in understanding this that I often think of another passage, Plotinus, another Friend of Time:

'The mind sheds radiance on the objects of sense, out of its own store.'

If a culture has in its store my figure—that moving figure assigned to me—my work is immediately recognized. It's heartwarming for me to exhibit in those places.

PHOTO: *Marlene M. Bell, award-winning author and artist, at her East Texas sheep ranch, where inspiration for her beloved stories begins.*

Exploring the World of

MARLENE M. BELL

Mysteries, Sheep, and Stories of the Heart

Marlene M. Bell discusses her acclaimed Annalisse series, the influence of her sheep ranch on her writing, and her creative process across mystery novels and children's books.

AS TOLD TO BEN ALAN

Literature

Marlene M. Bell is a literary for- ce whose work spans across genres, captivating readers of all ages with her vivid storytelling and rich character develop-ment. Her Annalisse series has gar-nered significant acclaim, with Copper Waters standing out as a masterful exploration of family ties and betrayal set against the breath-taking backdrop of New Zealand. Bell's ability to weave intricate plots with relatable characters is a testament to her skill as a writer. Her talents are not confined to adult fiction; her children's picture book, Mia and Nattie: One Great Team!, is a heart-warming tale inspired by

true events from her East Texas sheep ranch. This touching story of belonging and unconditional love between a little girl and her lamb has resonated with young readers and their families. Marlene's dedication to her craft and her ability to connect with audiences of all ages make her a standout figure in contemporary literature.

In this interview, we delve into the inspirations behind Marlene's work, her creative process, and the wisdom she offers to aspiring writers. From her intri-guing settings and complex charac-ters to her seamless integration of personal experiences into

her narratives, Marlene shares insights that reveal the depth of her passion for storytelling. Her journey from artist and photog-rapher to award-winning author is a testament to her multifaceted creativity and relentless pursuit of excellence. Join us as we explore the mind of Marlene M. Bell, a true luminary in the world of literature.

Your Annalisse series has gained significant acclaim, par-ticularly Copper Waters, which explores themes of family ties and betrayal. What inspired you to set this mystery in New Zealand, and how did the

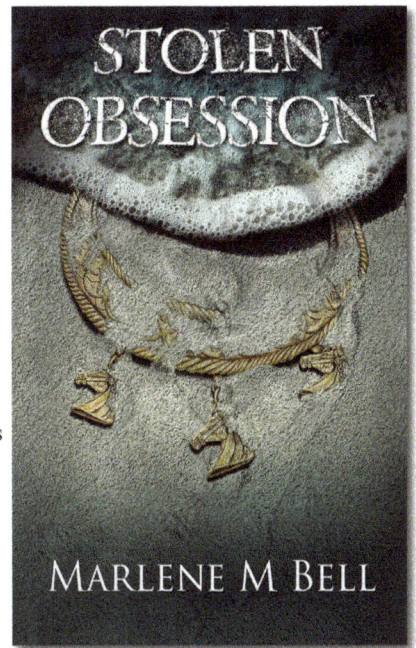

STOLEN OBSESSION

MARLENE M BELL

setting influence the development of the story?

Because of my sheep husbandry background, New Zealand was chosen for its beautiful scenic landscape and a place to showcase their sheep stations. Readers who might not know how other countries raise their sheep would find the information interesting and an excellent learning experience. This New Zealand getaway was necessary for my main characters to have time apart to work out their differences.

In A Hush at Midnight, the protagonist Laura Harris is a former celebrity chef entangled in a murder investigation. How do you go about creating such complex characters, and what role does the culinary world play in heightening the tension and intrigue in the story?

Another personal pastime of mine is cooking from scratch using fresh ingredients for the best dining experience. I thought it would be a challenge to create a character who loves to cook (bake) and bring another book out with an international flair due to Laura's training in France at one of the best culinary schools in the world.

Sheep often make appearances in your books, including your children's picture book Mia and Nattie: One Great Team! How does your life on a sheep ranch influence your writing, and what draws you to incorporate these animals into your stories?

My company, Ewephoric, was created in 1985 due to the lack of merchandise available depicting sheep in the retail world. I'm an artist and decided to bring out my own sheep-related products which led me to include other artisan's sheep gifts in a printed catalog and online. My husband and I raise various sheep breeds and have for well over 40 years. Having sheep as part of our family has made it essential to create stories with sheep and lambs making cameo appearances in novels and children's books. You could say, I write what I know! Mia and Nattie is based on raising a bottle lamb in our home and how she became important to our sheep operation.

Your work spans both adult mystery novels and children's books. How do you approach the different challenges these genres present, and what do you enjoy most about writing for such diverse audiences?

Raising Natalie, our bottle lamb we called "Nattie," taught me several life lessons. Mia and Nattie covers several of these lessons important for young people to learn as they mature and enter society. When Nattie passed on at the age of 13, it hit me harder than expected. I felt compelled to get her story out to children and their parents. Writing novels gave me the courage to jump out of my genre comfort zone and try something new to work through the grief.

As an accomplished artist and photographer, how does your visual creativity intersect with your writing process? Do you find that your artistic background influences how you describe settings or develop the visual elements of your stories?

Without question my ability to draw and paint what I see in nature has made me better at de- scriptions for my books. Through purchasing coffee table books and the visuals they provide, I can see the international locations for how they actually look, giving the reader an accurate view for their mind's eye as they read my novels. I rarely use the internet for research and depend on people who have actually been to the locations I write about.

With multiple awards under your belt, what advice would you give to aspiring writers who are trying to find their voice and establish themselves in the competitive world of publishing?

I went the longer route and learned as I published each book. Ten long years for Stolen Obsession. The first book in the Annalisse series required a lot of research on how to write fiction and what readers expect in every genre. I did what Traditional Publishers do for their authors when offering them a publishing contract.

The best advice I can give new authors is to research the genre they plan to write and read, read, read the work of other authors both inside the genre and outside. Reading opens the flow of words and helps with writer's block. When I'm blocked at the blank page, the best medicine is to pick up

Ania Danylo discusses her theatre background, transition to children's literature, and the interplay between her roles as director, educator, and writer, highlighting her passion for storytelling and creative collaboration.

ANIA DANYLO
EXPLORING THE CREATIVE WORLD
OF A MULTIFACETED ARTIST

Ania Danylo is a multifaceted talent whose contributions to the world of theatre and literature have left an indelible mark. With over 25 years of experience as an actor, director, writer, and instructor, Ania has brought to life a diverse array of productions, from the poignant *"The Diary of Anne Frank"* to the timeless enchantment of Shakespeare's *"A Midsummer Night's Dream."* Her directorial prowess extends to a variety of Shakespearean plays and other classics, showcasing her ability to navigate complex narratives and bring out the best in her cast and crew. Ania's dedication to the arts is further exemplified by her role as an educator, where she has inspired countless students to achieve their own successes, many of whom have gone on to win awards for their performances.

Ania's foray into children's literature is a testament to her storytelling prowess. Her books, *"The Elephant's Christmas Wish"* and *"Zolemina: The Should Do, Could Do, Would Do Cat,"* are delightful rhyming tales that capture the imagination of young readers. These works reflect her deep understanding of narrative structure, character development, and emotional resonance; skills honed through her extensive theatre background. Ania's ability to weave engaging stories for children is reminiscent of the whimsical charm found in the works of Shel Silverstein and Jack Prelutsky, yet uniquely her own. Her books not only entertain but also offer coloring book versions, inviting children to interact with the stories in a creative and personal way. Ania Danylo's contributions to both theatre and literature continue to inspire and captivate audiences of all ages.

With over 20 years of experience in theatre, including directing plays like The Diary of Anne Frank and Shakespeare's works, how has your background in theatre influenced your approach to writing children's books like The Elephant's Christmas Wish?

Engaging in directing and acting in the theatre is all about the art of storytelling. Shakespeare was a genius at it. Understanding how to build tension, create conflicts, and craft satisfying resolutions is essential for creating compelling narratives in children's picture books. It also involves mastering character development, pacing, rhythm and timing, language and imagery, emotional resonance, and themes. But I am also influenced by Shel Silverstein and Jack Prelutsky as much as I am by Shakespeare, Tennessee Williams, or Edward Albee. Directing also fosters attention to detail and the ability to see the big picture. Theatre, being a very visual and auditory medium, strongly connects with children's picture books.

When I initially wrote "The Elephant's Christmas Wish" as a poem, I envisioned it as a TV animation special rather than a book. I took it to

"

Ania Danylo, celebrated theatre director and children's author, shares her passion for storytelling and creativity.

AS TOLD TO DAN PETRES

a pitchfest many years ago and found a producer that would produce it if I could find a network to air it. Amazingly, I found a network to air it at the same pitchfest, but they wanted me to turn it into a 1-hour special or a 2-hour movie. At the time, I didn't know how to do that. But I am confident I could do it now.

It really wasn't until I read the poem to one of my adult acting students who said to me, "Why am I not reading this as a book to my grandkids at Christmas?" I thought, "Oh, I can make this a children's picture book." And so I did.

You've worked as both an acting instructor and a director for various theatre companies, including Storybook Theatre in Calgary. How do you balance the roles of educator, director, and writer, and how do these different aspects of your career inform each other?

As someone who's passionate about storytelling in all its forms, I've been fortunate to have had the opportunity to wear multiple hats in the world of theatre and writing. Balancing the roles of educator, director, and writer can be challenging, but I've found that each aspect informs and enriches the others in wonderful ways.

Ania Danylo is a visionary storyteller whose diverse talents enrich theatre and literature, inspiring audiences and students alike.

Your children's book, The Elephant's Christmas Wish, tells a story of perseverance and following one's dreams. What inspired you to write this story, and how do the themes of the book reflect your own experiences in the arts?

I have always been a firm believer in following dreams. It is hard to work in the arts if you don't believe in that. I also really liked elephants. In the past, I wrote a lot of interactive children's plays, which I produced and toured around Calgary and western Canada. Many of them were Christmas stories, which also held themes of following dreams and inclusion. When I got tired of touring and carrying my sets on my back with my small group of actors that I had assembled, I guess I had another Christmas story in me.

I also think part of the story came from one Christmas performance that we did in a local community where the audience was extremely diversified ethnically. I had been asked to drop all

of the "Christmas" references for that performance, which I thought was very odd based on the name of the play and the time of year.

When we arrived, I asked the person in charge if they really wanted us to lose Santa, the Elves, and all "Christmas" references. She looked horrified and said,Heck no, this is a Christmas party." It struck me funny that someone had assumed, because of their ethnicity, that the audience didn't want to celebrate Christmas at a, well, Christmas party. I have come across that a few times over the years. So, it struck me one day that an elephant might want to be part of Christmas too.

When I'm working on a project, I often find myself drawing on skills from each of these roles. For example, when writing a picture book, I might think like a director, imagining how the story would be staged or visualized. As an educator, I consider how the story can be used to teach or inspire young readers.

In terms of specific tips for balancing these roles, I've found it essential to prioritize my time, set clear goals, and be flexible. Some days, I'll focus on teaching or directing, while others are dedicated to writing. By allowing myself to oscillate between these roles, I've found that each one enriches the others, and I'm able to bring a unique perspective to each project.

You've also moved into the world of film and television, working on independent productions, commercials, and TV shows. What challenges did you face transitioning from theatre to screen, and how have these experiences shaped your creative process?

Transitioning from theatre to screen has had a few challenges as well as insights along the way.

I like to explain the fundamental differences most simply, as theatre is like talking into a megaphone (everything expands out) and film is like turning the megaphone backwards (everything contracts in). Film, by the very nature of the medium, is vastly more visual and less dependent on the spoken word. A great deal can be conveyed on the screen with the smallest of gestures, the twitch of a lip, or a glimpse of an eye. For the actor of film, the eyes are by far the most important, both in what they show in the spirit, soul, and emotions of the character and also in what they reflect in what the character sees.

In the world of theatre you are fully immersed in the story and life of the

character for weeks and often months. When you perform, the audience is right there with you, becoming part of the performance and giving immediate feedback. There is an energy that passes between the performers and the audience, whether it be a traditional play, an interactive script, or even an improvisational performance; the audience is an intrinsic element. The storyline is front and center through the rehearsals, and the performance is always beginning, middle, and end.

Film is very fragmented. The story is broken down into individual shots and scenes. While there may be numerous takes of the shots, the rehearsal process is not the same at all as in theatre. The team is much larger, with numerous crew members. The actor needs to quickly focus on the immediate scene, which is probably being shot well out of sequence of the storyline, as films are shot with the idea of keeping the costs as low as possible. Also, there is no energy between actors and audience since the audience comes much later. While actors and directors in films need to be story-focused as well, it really seems to me that the story itself becomes strongly defined by the editor, which is one of the most critical roles in filmmaking.

As a certified hypnotherapist and an experienced acting coach, you have a unique perspective on the mind and emotions. How do you incorporate these skills into your teaching and directing, and how do they help your students and actors achieve their best performances?

As a certified hypnotherapist and experienced acting coach, I've had the privilege of delving into the inner workings of the mind and emotions. I've discovered that these skills are invaluable in helping my students and actors access their full potential and deliver truly captivating performances. There are many tools, such as visualization, body mirroring, etc., that can be useful for producing great performances; however, the very best one is to "be specific."

But truly the most important part of my teaching, coaching, and therapy is providing a very relaxed atmosphere coupled with a fair amount of humor. Providing a safe environment where actors feel comfortable to take risks, try out ideas, push the boundaries, and, yes, laughing brilliantly when things

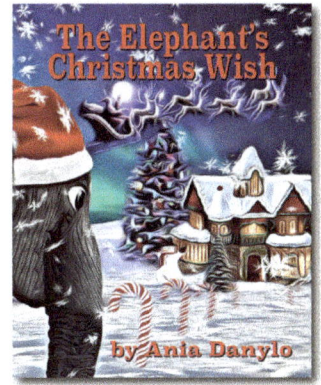

A heartwarming tale of perseverance and inclusion, beautifully illustrated, capturing the spirit of Christmas through an elephant's adventurous journey.

don't quite work out, goes a very long way to building confidence. Confidence is key to a good actor, public speaker, and/or storyteller. I always tell my actors and students that the most important part of their job is to have fun. Having fun is contagious. I like to think all performances possess the power of passion and the fragrance and flavor of fun.

Your book features 56 illustrations by Remi Bryant. How did you collaborate with the illustrator to bring Felix the elephant and his journey to life visually, and what was the process like of turning your written story into a fully illustrated children's book?

Remi was fantastic to work with. She not only did the illustrations but also mentored me in how to self-publish a book, which I knew nothing about. But I was a pain in the butt, you know? Before hiring Remi, I actually completed three iterations of my own version of the book, so I knew precisely what I wanted in terms of style. I therefore had some very strong thoughts right away, and she did a terrific job of collecting copious notes from me throughout. That is something that carried over very strongly with me from my years of directing. I can always see how to tweak something just a bit more to make it just a bit better. Without a doubt, I am sure I drove her more than a bit crazy. Plus, I was traveling through Bulgaria when we worked on a lot of the book, so the time differences were quite challenging. But she was fantastic to work with and learn from.

But given the high cost of printing, 56 full-color illustrations for a book is just absurd. When I began writing "Zolemina: The Should Do Could Do Would Do Cat," my second children's book, I started with it in mind. I did manage to get my page count down from 56 illustrations. But I was having

so much fun collaborating with my illustrator, David Griffiths, that I wasn't able to stick to my goal of 32.Thus, I also converted both stories to coloring books. While black and white pages are more economical to print, coloring them inspires children's innate desire for self-expression. The surprise was people were buying extra coloring books for their grandparents and elderly relatives. BEAUTY PRIME II 51

Exploring the Depths of Human Emotion

Dr. Eichin Chang-Lim discusses her diverse career's influence on her writing, exploring themes of love, mental health, and personal growth through authentic, multidimensional characters and emotionally resonant narratives.

"

Dr. Eichin Chang-Lim, a multi-awarded author, draws inspiration from her diverse career to craft emotionally resonant and intellectually stimulating stories.

AS TOLD TO BEN ALAN

EICHIN CHANG-LIM
THE MULTIFACETED WORLD
OF DR. CHANG-LIM

Dr. Eichin Chang-Lim's acclaimed works explore love, mental health, and personal growth, offering readers profound insights into the human experience.

Dr. Eichin Chang-Lim is a remarkable figure whose multifaceted career spans the realms of optometry, acting, and writing. Her diverse background enriches her story-telling, allowing her to craft narratives that are both intellectually stimulating and emotionally resonant. As a multi-awarded author, Dr. Chang-Lim has made significant contributions to literature across various genres, captivating readers with her ability to weave complex characters and compelling plots. Her works, such as "*The LoveLock*" and "*Love: A Tangled Knot,*" delve into the intricacies of love and human relationships, while her memoir, "*A Mother's Heart: Memoir of a Special Needs Parent,*" offers a poignant and honest exploration of personal challenges and triumphs. Dr. Chang-Lim's dedication to exploring themes of love, mental health, and personal growth has earned her a well-deserved place in the literary world, and her stories continue to inspire and resonate with readers around the globe.

In this insightful interview, Dr. Chang-Lim shares how her varied experiences have shaped her writing and influenced her understanding of human emotions and relationships. Her unique perspective, drawn from her professional and personal life, allows her to create authentic and relatable characters that connect with readers on a profound level. Join us as we delve into the mind of this extraordinary author, exploring the themes and motivations behind her acclaimed works and gaining a deeper understanding of the stories that have touched the hearts of many.

Your diverse career includes optometry, acting, and writing across multiple genres. How do these varied experiences influence your writing, particularly in crafting multidimensional characters and emotionally resonant narratives?

My career in optometry, acting, and writing has profoundly shaped my approach to crafting complex, relatable characters. Op-

"Talking About Adolescence" is an insightful guide that compassionately addresses teen mental health, offering practical advice and fostering understanding for both parents and adolescents.

Book 1
Anxiety, Depression, and Adolescent Mental Health

TALKING ABOUT
ADOLESCENCE

Eichin Chang-Lim, OD, MS, MA &
Lara L. Erickson, PhD, LCPC, LMHC-QS, LPC

How to Navigate through Adolescence Successfully and Have a Happy Life

tometry connected me with diverse people, offering insights into their hopes, fears, and vulnerabilities. Acting honed my ability to embody different personas and explore human emotion. These experiences congregate in my writing, enabling me to create characters with authenticity and emotional resonance that connect with readers across cultures. This blend of scientific precision, artistic expression, and storytelling allows me to craft narratives that are entertaining, emotional, and intellectually stimulating.

In a recent interview, you emphasized that love is multidimensional and involves aspects like sacrifice, forgiveness, and trust. Can you elaborate on how these themes manifest in your novels, especially in The LoveLock and Love: A Tangled Knot?

Both LoveLock and Love: A Tangled Knot explore love's multidimensional nature, highlighting sacrifice, forgiveness, and trust. These stories depict love as a force that intertwines souls, elevates the human spirit, and transcends time, space and circumstances, emphasizing commitment, endurance, and hope. They present a comprehensive picture of love, encompassing sibling bonds, family ties, friendships, and pet relationships. Love is not just about intimacy and passion; it is about elevating others and enduring life's trials. These books highlight the importance of compassion and warmth, illustrating how various forms of love shape our lives and enrich the human experience.

Your memoir, A Mother's Heart: Memoir of a Special Needs Parent, provides a raw and honest look at the challenges and triumphs of raising a child with special needs. What motivated you to share this deeply personal journey, and what do you hope readers will take away from your story?

In A Mother's Heart, I illuminate the often-hidden world of raising a

child with special needs. My memoir offers offering hope, support, and practical insights. By sharing my experiences, I aim to break down stigma, empower parents, and promote a sense of community. My message is clear: never give up. Your strength can empower your child to thrive. Hold tight to hope!

Your Precious Sight highlights memorable cases from your career as an optometrist. How did you decide which stories to include, and what impact do you hope this book has on both medical professionals and the general public?

My primary goal in writing Your Precious Sight was to educate the public about eye health. I selected common and relevant cases, presenting them in a storytelling format to make complex medical issues relatable. Through these engaging stories, I emphasize the crucial role of regular eye exams in detecting insidious diseases like glaucoma early, thereby preventing blindness. Ultimately, the book seeks to demystify eye health, raise awareness, and empower readers to take proactive steps in caring for their vision.

You mentioned that you strive to write stories that go beyond the confines of romance, encompassing the love of friendship, family, and pets. How do you approach balancing these different forms of love in your novels to create a holistic and relatable portrayal of human relationships?

In my novels, I envision love as a multifaceted gem, capturing its brilliance in all its forms. Drawing from my life experiences, I explore the complexities of romantic relationships, familial bonds, and friendships. The interplay of family support, unwavering friendships, and unconditional love from animals enriches the human experience and brings characters to life. By depicting these diverse relationships, I aim to create authentic and relatable characters that inspire readers to cherish and celebrate the richness of

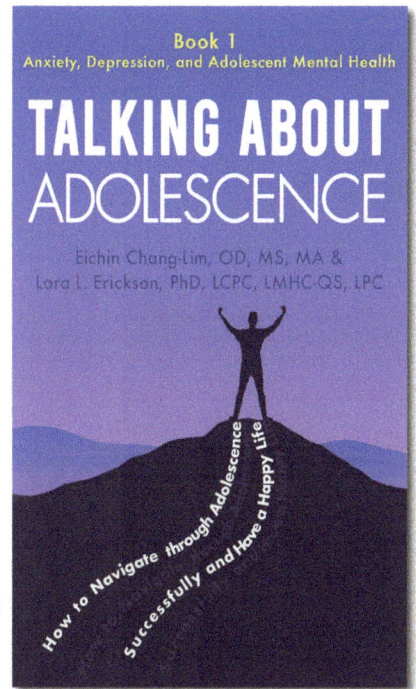

all human interactions.

Mental health and overcoming personal challenges are significant themes in your books, such as in The LoveLock and Talking About Adolescence: Anxiety, Depression, and Adolescent Mental Health. How do your personal and professional experiences shape your understanding of these issues, and what message do you aim to convey to your readers through these narratives?

As an optometrist, I have seen how unique life experiences shape our perceptions and affect our mental and physical well-being. Adverse events can leave lasting imprints, influencing our thoughts, behaviors, and social relationships. Through my narratives, I highlight the profound impact of mental health and the connection between the mind and body.

Key messages in my writing include:

Seek Help: Never let stigma prevent you from seeking support. Asking for help is a sign of strength.

No Shame: Mental illness is not your fault, and there is nothing to be ashamed of.

Hope and Healing: Recovery from traumatic experiences is possible with support. Hold on to faith and hope.

I aim to create an inclusive world that prioritizes mental well-being and makes mental health accessible to everyone.

Dr. Eichin Chang-Lim masterfully blends intellect and emotion, creating compelling narratives that resonate deeply with readers across diverse genres.

Learn more about
Dr. Eichin Chang-Lim
https://eichinchanglim.com

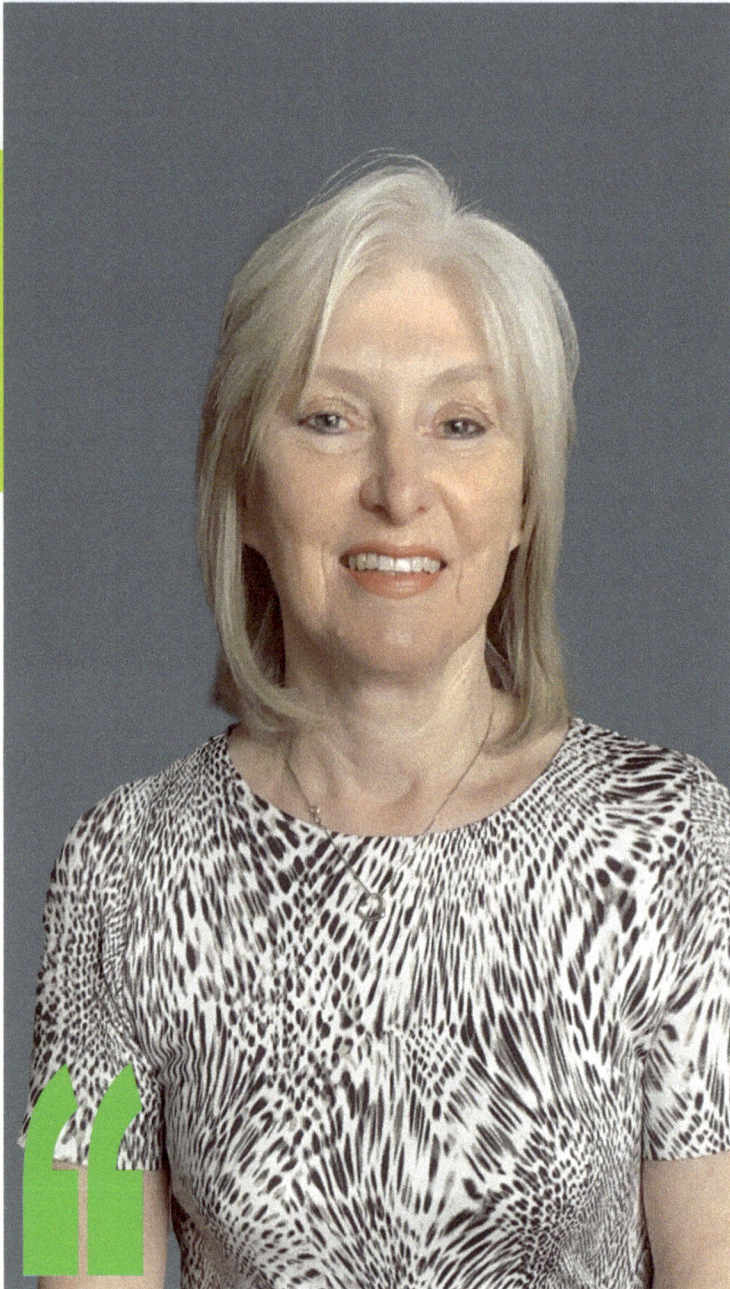

From Australia to the Forest of Dean

Cheryl Burman blends her Australian roots and life in the Forest of Dean to create award-winning historical fiction and fantasy, captivating readers with rich, diverse narratives.

CHERYL BURMAN

HOW DIVERSE SETTINGS AND GENRES SHAPE THE STORIES OF AN AWARD-WINNING AUTHOR

AS TOLD TO BEN ALAN

Cheryl Burman, a literary talent with roots in both Australia and the Forest of Dean, UK, has carved a unique niche in the world of historical fiction and fantasy. Her diverse background and rich experiences have infused her writing with a depth and authenticity that resonates with readers across the globe. Burman's impressive portfolio includes two award-winning historical fiction novels, one of which has achieved bestseller status on US Amazon, alongside two novellas and a captivating fantasy series for younger audiences. Her short stories and flash fiction, celebrated for their narrative prowess, have found homes in various collections and anthologies.

A dedicated student of the writing craft, Burman shares her insights through articles and a popular blog, guiding aspiring writers with her expertise. Under the name Cheryl Mayo, she has also played a pivotal role in nurturing local literary talent as the former chair of the Dean Writers Circle and a founder of Dean Scribblers, a group dedicated to fostering creative writing among young people in her community.

In this interview, Cheryl Burman opens up about the profound influence of her Australian heritage and her life in the Forest of Dean on her storytelling. She discusses the inspiration behind her diverse genres, the development of beloved characters like Alf from "Walking in

Cheryl Burman, acclaimed author, at her home in the Forest of Dean, where she draws inspiration for her captivating stories.

Literature

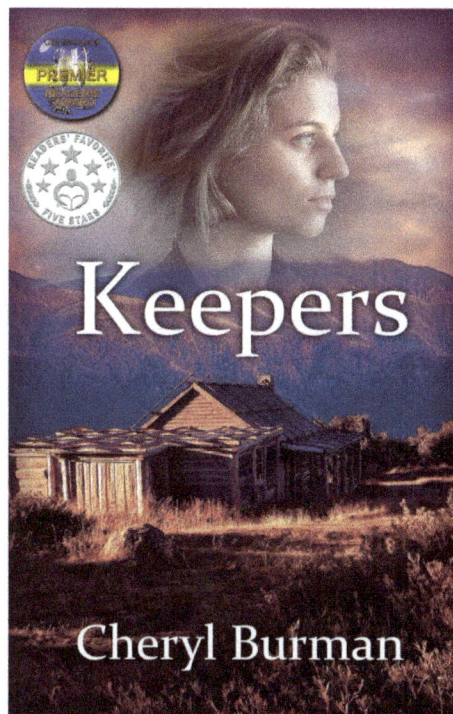

Keepers

Cheryl Burman

the Rain," and the historical and mythical elements that enrich her narratives. Burman also reflects on her work with young writers and offers valuable advice to those embarking on their own literary journeys. Join us as we delve into the mind of a writer who seamlessly blends history, myth, and personal struggle to create stories that captivate and inspire.

Your experiences in both Australia and the *Forest of Dean* have significantly influenced your writing. How do these diverse settings inspire the themes and characters in your stories?

Readers are often told to 'write what we know'. While Australia

and the Forest are indeed diverse settings, they are both places I love and are familiar with, and each provides a deep well to draw on. They are, however, different wells.

As the country where I was born and grew up, I burrowed deeply into memories of places and people from my childhood in Australia for my women's fiction novel Keepers and its two spinoffs. Set in post world war two Australia, the story is loosely based on family lore, weaving real events into a dramatic tale. I had fun playing fast and loose with the personalities of friends and family, creating new characters, and placing the combined cast into historical places they may or may not have visited.

The Forest of Dean provides a different, more vicarious,

inspiration given I moved here relatively late in life. This is a place full of history, legend and ancient traditions, and a landscape scattered with the remains of a fascinating past. It's these secondhand experiences which whisper a hundred stories in my willing ears.

From middle-grade fantasy to historical fantasy, your writing spans multiple genres. What motivates you to explore such diverse literary landscapes, and how do you approach the challenge of switching between genres?

I've been an avid and eclectic reader of fiction since childhood. So while I started writing with middle grade fantasy, I saw no reason why that should be my only genre, just as I wouldn't read only one type of book. Switching between genres is not a challenge for me, but an opportunity to tell a new story in a way appropriate to that story and its target audience. I have much to draw on as examples. Having said that, over time I've developed a style of my own – what authors call 'voice' – and this can work as a unifying factor. It makes life easier for me, and it helps my readers feel comfortable that this is 'another Cheryl book' and therefore they are likely to enjoy it whatever the genre.

Your latest work, *Walking in the Rain*, delves into themes of love, regret, and second chances. What inspired Alf's journey, and how did you develop his character throughout the series?

Dear Alf, everyone loves him. In fact, it was Alf's situation at the end of Keepers which led to Walking in the Rain – many fans were outraged at his fate! Alf's journey from being Teddy's

self-sacrificing side-kick to finding his own true happiness was a delight to write. His fumbling honesty with Raine, and how she responds, his ongoing inner turmoil and, finally, his decision to stop moping and get a life of his own, has endeared Alf to many. His character arc needed to be steady and thoughtful, taking time and with some backward steps, as he worked his way through his self-doubts to that 'lightbulb' moment.

In *River Witch*, Hester battles societal expectations and personal ambitions in 19th-century England. What drew you to write about this historical period and the themes of witchcraft and empowerment?

The story behind River Witch fell into my lap when I was asked to edit a non-fiction account of a Forest of Dean woman tried for witchcraft in 1906 (yes, 1906). My initial intention was to write a biographical novel, but the research was thin. As a lover of magical realism, I decided to combine elements of myth and legend from the Forest and go with historical fantasy instead. Much more fun! So the true story inspired the witchy vibes. The empowerment? That fell out of the tale as I wrote it, as did other themes such as resilience and reconciliation.

As a founder of Dean Scribblers, you encourage young people to explore creative writing. How has this experience influenced your own writing, and what advice would you give to aspiring young authors?

Helping young people craft a story is always a joy. In terms of my own writing, it's shown me that kids as young as ten have a

good grasp of the realities of the world (a little sad), tend to be a tad bloodthirsty and at the same time can portray deep emotion. It means I don't need to be bland when writing for middle graders!

My advice to them? Keep writing.

Your novels often weave elements of history, myth, and personal struggle. How do you balance these components to create engaging and relatable narratives for your readers?

All readable fiction is about personal struggle, 'the hero's journey'. In fact, one piece of advice I do give young people is to throw as many obstacles as possible in your character's path and see how they cope. But writers and readers have preferences for different settings of the tale: fantasy, historical, romcom, women's fiction etc.

History and myth provide the backdrops to my stories. But more than that, they also drive the way characters behave and make choices, and thus they inform their struggles. In Keepers, the social mores of 1951 dictated Raine and Teddy's behaviour and triggered the whole messy tale. Similar, River Witch is a story of the time's prejudices and their impact on Hester.

Relevance is key for a relatable narrative – characters must be believable in their setting.

Master of Suspense and Storytelling

J.T. Ellison, bestselling author, blends crime, suspense, and fantasy in her novels. Her diverse background and disciplined approach create compelling stories that captivate readers worldwide.

J.T. ELLISON

EXPLORING CRIME, FANTASY, AND COLLABORATION WITH A LITERARY POWERHOUSE

AS TOLD TO BEN ALAN

J.T. Ellison is a literary force to be reckoned with. As a New York Times and USA Today bestselling author, she has penned over 30 critically acclaimed novels that span the thrilling spectrum of crime, suspense, and psychological tension. Her standalone works, such as "A Very Bad Thing" and "It's One of Us," alongside her gripping series featuring Lt. Taylor Jackson and Dr. Samantha Owens, have captivated readers worldwide. Not only has she co-authored the "A Brit in the FBI" series with Catherine Coulter, but she has also ventured into the realm of urban fantasy under the pen name Joss Walker, creating the enchanting Jayne Thorne, CIA Librarian series.

Ellison's journey to literary stardom is as compelling as her novels. From her early days in the foothills of Colorado to her high-stakes career in Washington, D.C., and eventually to her life in Nashville, her diverse experiences have profoundly shaped her storytelling. Her fascination with forensics and crime, coupled with her disciplined approach honed in the political arena, has given rise to a body of work that is both meticulously crafted and deeply engaging.

Beyond her writing, Ellison is an Emmy® Award-winning co-host of the television series "A Word on Words," where she delves into the minds of fellow authors, exploring the intricacies of their craft. Her passion for literature extends to publishing, with her independent house, Two Tales Press, showcasing a variety of short stories and novellas.

"

J.T. Ellison, the acclaimed author behind numerous bestselling thrillers and fantasy novels, continues to captivate readers with her compelling storytelling.

In this exclusive interview for Reader's House Magazine, J.T. Ellison opens up about her transition from politics to writing, the allure of dark themes, the dynamics of co-authoring, and the creative freedoms of fantasy. She also shares insights into her literary television show and the diverse settings that color her novels. Join us as we delve into the mind of one of today's most versatile and prolific authors.

Your journey to becoming a bestselling author is both fascinating and unconventional, involving a significant career change from politics to writing. What was the most challenging part of making that transition, and how did your previous experiences shape your writing?

It was one of necessity—we'd moved to Nashville and I couldn't find a job! A librarian turned me on to John Sandford, and it was like a lightning bolt—I decided to write an incredibly heroic female lead who was a half cop, half rockstar, the

J.T. Ellison's masterful storytelling and versatile writing make her a standout author in both thriller and fantasy genres.

guardian angel of Nashville—my very own Athena. Taylor Jackson was born.

The political world taught me one very important trait: discipline. Congress (and your boss) don't take kindly to missing your white paper deadlines. I learned how to budget my time and take the work seriously, and I applied that to the creative side.

Your novels often explore dark and thrilling themes. What draws you to write about crime, suspense, and psychological tension, and how do you balance these elements with character development to keep readers engaged?

I am fascinated by how terrible people can be to one another, and I like to see justice served in some way. Too often, cases go

unsolved and families are torn apart. When I write thrillers, I'm always imagining what's happening on the other side of the door. If it's a procedural, my character knocks on the doors. If it's suspense, the character's door is knocked upon. It gives me a deeper perspective on the emotional frailty of the characters.

In addition to your standalone thrillers, you've co-authored a successful series with Catherine Coulter. How does the collaboration process work for you, and what are the unique challenges and rewards of co-writing compared to working solo?

Cowriting is a lot of fun and can also be hugely challenging. You know the saying "two heads are better than one." If I ever got stuck, help was a phone call or a plane ride away. Catherine and I worked well together because we had the same work ethic, which is absolutely vital to the co-writing process. You can't put two writers together who don't see the process of writing the same way. But it was the brainstorming, the wild twists we came up with, that was the most fun—creativity blossoms when there are two minds on a story.

Your alter ego, Joss Walker, writes contemporary fantasy. How do you switch between writing in the thriller genre and fantasy, and what creative freedoms does the fantasy genre offer you that thrillers might not?

Fantasy is my one true love right now, mostly because if you get into a bind…magic! The brilliant Raymond Chandler has a straightforward solution: "When in doubt, have a man come through a door with a gun in his hand." In fantasy, the ability to conjure a solution is a blast. I also love worldbuilding with no fetters on the imagination. You are only limited by how big of a canvas you can conceive. It helps me breathe fresh air into my crime fiction.

You're an Emmy® award-winning co-host of the literary TV show A Word on Words. How has hosting this show influenced

your own writing and perspective on literature, and what has been your most memorable moment on the show?

I've gotten to read more broadly, which never hurts. Experiencing new genres, cultures, diverse voices, and other authors' life experiences is as beneficial as traveling for me. Meeting these incredible artists, seeing their creative process, and discovering the spark of their ideas has been incredibly fun.

There have been many special moments over the past ten seasons, but I have to say, going to jail with Margaret Atwood has to be number one. The producers literally put us in a jail cell and locked the door for the taping. She was such a good sport.

Your personal background, from growing up in rural Colorado to working in high-stakes political environments, is quite diverse. How do these contrasting experiences influence the settings and characters in your novels, and do you have a particular favorite setting you've written about?

At heart, I am a country mouse, though I enjoy the bustling big city, and my settings reflect that. Nashville is the connective tissue through all of my work, but I've also written books set in Colorado and DC because they are so easily accessible to me. I travel quite a bit to broaden my horizons, too. The UK, France, and Italy are favorites; all have featured heavily in my stories. I have a research trip to Scotland this fall, and I can't wait. There's something special about the UK; stories tug at my legs as I walk the paths. Its own source of magic.

Thank you for having me! This was fun!

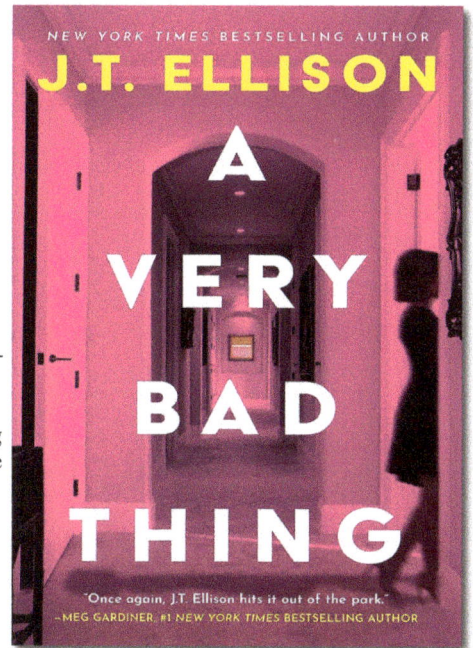

NEW YORK TIMES BESTSELLING AUTHOR
J.T. ELLISON
A VERY BAD THING

"Once again, J.T. Ellison hits it out of the park."
—MEG GARDINER, #1 NEW YORK TIMES BESTSELLING AUTHOR

A Very Bad Thing is a masterful thriller, brimming with suspense, intricate plot twists, and unforgettable characters. An absolute must-read!

Exploring the Journey

Thomas White's diverse career spans acting, directing, and writing. His novels, inspired by historical events and personal experiences, captivate readers with imaginative storytelling and emotional depth.

as told to J. Evans

Master Storyteller Across Mediums

Thomas White's journey from the theater to the literary world is a testament to the power of storytelling in all its forms. Beginning his career as an actor, White quickly transitioned to directing, earning accolades such as Drama-Logue and Critics awards. His role as Artistic Director for a Los Angeles theater set the stage for his future endeavors, including the world tour of "*The Teenage Mutant Ninja Turtles: Coming Out Of Their Shells,*" which captivated nearly a million children worldwide. With a career spanning over two decades as President and Creative Director of Maiden Lane Entertainment, White has orchestrated large-scale corporate events for giants like Harley Davidson and Microsoft. Now, as an acclaimed author, he continues to weave compelling narratives, with his latest novel, "The Edison Enigma," adding to his growing literary repertoire.

White's diverse background in theater and event production has profoundly influenced his approach to writing. "*As a director, you tell stories using actors, sets, props, and lighting. As an author, you use your words,*" he explains. This seamless transition from stage to page underscores his belief that the core objective remains the same: to engage the audience emotionally. Whether through a theatrical production or a novel, White's goal is to captivate and entertain, ensuring that the audience remains invested from beginning to end.

The Edison Enigma, White's third novel, delves into the intriguing concept of time travel and the consequences of altering history. The inspiration for this theme came from a corporate event for Saturn in 1997, where the electric car, the EV-1, was unveiled. Years later, an article titled "The Death Of The Electric Car" sparked White's curiosity about the historical trajectory of electric vehicles. His research revealed a series of coincidences at the turn of the 20th century, leading him to imagine a scenario where the world chose electric cars over internal combustion engines. This imaginative leap forms the crux of *The Edison Enigma,* blending science fiction with historical speculation to create a thought-provoking narrative.

In *The Siren's Scream,* White explores the eerie Thornton Mansion and its mysterious tide pool, a setting that exudes suspense and dread. Initially inspired by mermaid myths, White sought to breathe new life into the well-worn trope. The idea of mermaids dealing with familial conflicts and lineage sparked a storyline that evolved into a gripping tale of mystery and intrigue. By reimagining the mermaid mythos, White crafted a novel that stands out in the genre, offering readers a fresh perspective on an ancient legend.

Justice Rules, White's debut novel, centers on FBI Special Agent Brian Wylie and a vigilante coalition. The plot was inspired by the aftermath of the OJ Simpson trial, particularly the emotional devastation of Ron Goldman's father, Fred. This poignant moment led White to ponder the lengths one might go to seek justice outside the legal system. The resulting narrative explores themes of justice and morality, challenging readers to consider the complexities of revenge and retribution.

Recognition as a finalist in the Pacific Northwest Writers Association 2010 Literary contest for "Justice Rules" was a significant milestone in White's writing career. Although he did not immediately follow up with another novel, the nomination affirmed his talent and potential as a writer. Reflecting on the experience, White acknowledges the honour but also the overwhelming nature of his accomplishment, which led to a decade-long hiatus before his next literary endeavor.

Balancing the creative demands of writing novels with the logistical challenges of producing events is no small feat, yet White finds parallels between the two processes. "*I always describe my career as being someone in production,*" he says. Whether producing plays, corporate events, or novels, the skill set remains consistent: envisioning a project and bringing it to life. The blank page, much like an empty stage, represents both a challenge and an opportunity for creativity to flourish.

Thomas White's multifaceted career exemplifies the versatility and resilience of a true storyteller. From the theater to the corporate world and now to the realm of literature, his ability to engage and entertain remains unwavering. As he continues to craft new narratives, readers can look forward to more captivating tales from this accomplished author.

Thomas White's storytelling prowess and creative versatility make him a standout author, seamlessly blending history, imagination, and emotion.

" *I always describe my career as being someone in production. I produce plays, musicals, sales events, corporate meetings, product reveals, novels, etc. The skill set is pretty much the same, you create a vision in your head, then utilize your skill set to make it come to life. Writer's always talk about the blank piece of paper and how there is nothing scarier. That is 100% true.*

Thomas White

Why Financial Planning Is a Great Career Option for Women

Financial planning is an increasingly popular and lucrative career for women, offering high salaries, work-life balance, personal fulfillment, and strong support networks, including initiatives, scholarships, and mentorships from the CFP Board.

as told to J. Evans

Financial planning was once thought of as a male-dominated industry, but that's quickly changing. The number of women getting their CERTIFIED FINANCIAL PLANNER™ certification is growing year over year — and for good reason: The benefits of entering this field as a woman are numerous. Below are a few to consider.

• It's lucrative. Financial planners are in high demand and are well-compensated for their expertise. A financial advisor can pull in a generous salary right out of the gate, and earning the right credentials can boost compensation significantly. The median income for those with CFP® certification and less than 5 years of experience is $100,000 — and that median figure grows to $206,000 with 10 or more years of experience. In general, financial advisors with CFP® certification earn 12% more than those without.

• Being a CFP® professional offers good work-life balance. With the potential to work remotely and create one's own schedule, financial planning is a career path well-suited to those looking for flexibility and a desirable work-life balance.

• Financial planning can be personally fulfilling. Providing competent, ethical financial advice that helps others achieve their life goals — from sending their children to college to securing a comfortable retirement — can be extremely gratifying.

Research also finds that female CFP® professionals have a unique dedication to providing holistic financial planning. Working as a financial planner provides opportunities to uplift and empower other women, as well as members of groups historically given fewer opportunities to accumulate wealth.

• Women who aspire to become CFP® professionals will find support in many places. CFP Board, for example, has implemented initiatives to recruit women and advance their careers.

Some firms subsidize the cost of CFP® certification and give employees time away from work to study for the CFP® exam. Additionally, women's networks and business councils can help build leadership skills and professional confidence, and many firms are even paying their employees' membership fees.

CFP Board also administers scholarships for individuals underrepresented in the field, along with a mentoring program.

To learn more and get started today on your path to becoming a CFP® professional, visit getCFPcertified.org.

With demand for personal financial advisors expected to grow significantly in the coming years, and the industry making way for more women professionals, it's worth exploring this rewarding career path.

PHOTO SOURCE: monkeybusinessimages / iStock via Getty Images Plus (StatePoint)

Celebrating the Visionaries of Beauty

BEAUTY PRIME

beautyprime.co.uk
ISSUE 4 - 2024
GLOBAL EDITION

CONFIDENCE IS THE FOUNDATION OF TRUE BEAUTY

The Power Of Fashion And Makeup In Building Self-Confidence

PASCALE ROTHMAN
Redefines health with integrity, transparency, and innovation

MELINDA NICCI
Empowers Women Through Wellness

KRISTIAN EDWARDS
Empowers Wellness

Available in

PRINT

Americas to Australia

Europe to Africa Reader's House is available over 190 countries and thousands of retaiers, platforms including Amazon, Barnes & Noble, Walmart, Waterstone's .....

ELECTRONIC

It is an electronic (flip book) format and interactive. Accessable from electronic devices like pc, smart phone, notepads..

ONLINE

All interviews, we conduct make them accessable online for free.

SOCIAL MEDIA

We are on Facebook, Instagram and X. Please follow us on social media @beautyprimemag

contact us today for an interview opportunity at
editor@beautyprime.co.uk

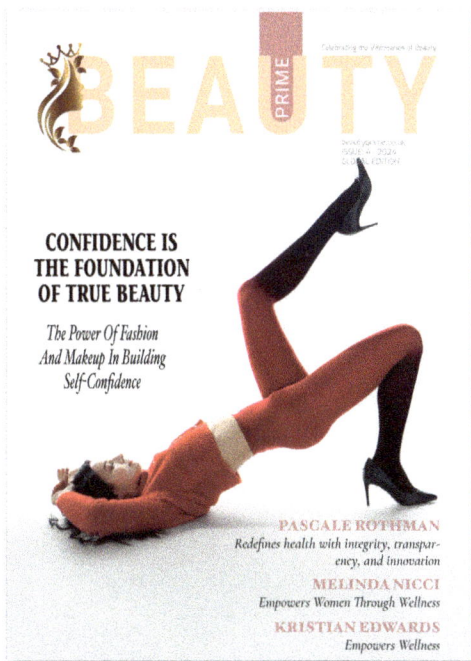

CONFIDENCE IS
THE FOUNDATION
OF TRUE BEAUTY

*The Power Of Fashion
And Makeup In Building
Self-Confidence*

PASCALE ROTHMAN
Redefines health with integrity, transparency, and innovation

MELINDA NICCI
Empowers Women Through Wellness

KRISTIAN EDWARDS
Empowers Wellness

Save up to 50% when you
order 10 or more from the
same issue

Subscribe Now!

YES! I would like a subscription to

☐ Current Issue for

☐ One-Year Subscription (_____ Issues) for

☐ Two-Year Subscription (_____ Issues) for

☐ I am a renewing a current subscription   ☐ I am a new subscriber

Name: _____ Phone: _____

Shipping Address: _____

Billing Address: _____

Email: _____

☐ Yes, I would like to receive updates, newsletters and special offers
☐ No, I would NOT like to receive updates, newsletters and special offers

Payment Type: ☐ Check   ☐ Bank transfer   ☐ Wise   ☐ PayPal

_____

_____

Please mail this form to:
Magazine Name:

www.ingramcontent.com/pod-product-compliance
Lightning Source LLC
Chambersburg PA
CBHW052348210326
41597CB00037B/6293